Reading Skills

Grade 5

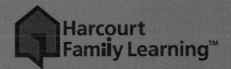

Harcourt Family Learning™

© 2004 by Flash Kids
Adapted from *Comprehension Skills Complete Classroom Library*
by Linda Ward Beech, Tara McCarthy, and Donna Townsend
© 2001 by Harcourt Achieve
Licensed under special arrangement with Harcourt Achieve.

Illustrator: Clive Scruton

ISBN: 978-1-4114-0117-4

Please submit all inquiries to FlashKids@bn.com

Printed and bound in China

Flash Kids
A Division of Barnes & Noble
122 Fifth Avenue
New York, NY 10011

Dear Parent,

The ability to read well is an important part of your child's development. This book is designed to help your child become a better reader. The wide range of high-interest stories will hold your child's attention and help develop his or her proficiency in reading. Each of the six units focuses on a different reading comprehension skill: finding facts, detecting a sequence, learning new vocabulary through context, identifying the main idea, drawing conclusions, and making inferences. Mastering these skills will ensure that your child has the necessary tools needed for a lifetime love of reading.

Unit 1 contains activities to fine-tune your child's ability to spot facts in a story—a necessary skill for understanding a reading selection. This unit is filled with stories to test your child's understanding of how to identify facts in a story. The focus is on specific details that tell who, what, when, where, and how.

Reading for sequence means identifying the order of events in a story or the steps in a process, and understanding the relationship of one event or step to other events or steps. Unit 2 contains stories that will test your child's understanding of the order of events in a story.

Unit 3 teaches your child how to use context to learn new words. When practicing using context, your child must use all the words in a reading selection to understand the unfamiliar words. This important skill helps a reader understand words and concepts by learning how language is used to express meaning. Mastering this skill ensures that your child will become a successful independent reader.

One of the keys to learning to read well is being able to differentiate between the main point of a reading selection and the supporting details. Unit 4 will help your child learn to recognize the main idea of a story.

Drawing a conclusion is a complex reading skill because a conclusion is not stated in a reading selection. Your child must learn to put together the details from the information as if they were clues to a puzzle. The conclusion must be supported by the details in the reading selection. Unit 5 contains stories to help your child learn to draw conclusions about the passages in the book.

To make an inference, your child must consider all the facts in a reading selection. Then he or she must put together those facts and what is already known to make a reasonable inference about something that is not stated in the selection. Making an inference requires the reader to go beyond the information in the text. Unit 6 will help your child learn how to make inferences.

To help your child get the most from this workbook, encourage your child to read each reading selection slowly and carefully. Explain the purpose of each unit to your child so that he or she has a better understanding of how it will help his or her reading skills. There's an answer key at the end of this workbook. Your child can check the answer key to see which questions he or she got right and wrong. Go back to the questions your child answered incorrectly and go over them again to see why he or she picked the incorrect answer. Completing the activities in this workbook will get your child on the right track to becoming an excellent reader. Continue your child's educational development at home with these fun activities:

- Enlist your child's help when writing grocery lists.
- When preparing a meal, have your child read the recipe aloud.
- Provide entertaining reading selections for your child. Have a discussion about what he or she has read.
- Instead of reading a bedtime story to your child, have your child read a bedtime story to you!
- Write down the directions to a project, such as a gardening project or an arts and crafts project, for your child to read.
- Give your child a fun reading passage and ask him or her to draw a picture about it.
- Ask your child to read road signs and billboards that you encounter during car trips.
- Leave cute notes on the refrigerator or your child's pillow.
- Have your child write and mail a letter to a loved one.
- Ask your child to read the directions for a board game, and then play the game together.
- Bring your child to the library or bookstore so that he or she can choose which great book to read next.

Table of Contents

unit 1
Facts

What Are Facts?	6
Practice Finding Facts	7
Lesson 1	8
Lesson 2	10
Lesson 3	12
Lesson 4	14
Lesson 5	16
Lesson 6	18
Lesson 7	20
Lesson 8	22
Writing Roundup	24

unit 2
Sequence

What Is Sequence?	26
Practice with Sequence	27
Lesson 1	28
Lesson 2	30
Lesson 3	32
Lesson 4	34
Lesson 5	36
Lesson 6	38
Lesson 7	40
Lesson 8	42
Writing Roundup	44

unit 3
Context

What Is Context?	46
Working with Context	47
Lesson 1	48
Lesson 2	50
Lesson 3	52
Lesson 4	54
Lesson 5	56
Lesson 6	58
Lesson 7	60
Lesson 8	62
Writing Roundup	64

unit 4
Main Idea

What Is a Main Idea? 66
Practice Finding the Main Idea 67
Lesson 1 68
Lesson 2 70
Lesson 3 72
Lesson 4 74
Lesson 5 76
Lesson 6 78
Lesson 7 80
Lesson 8 82
Writing Roundup 84

unit 5
Conclusion

What Is a Conclusion? 86
Using What You Know 87
Lesson 1 88
Lesson 2 90
Lesson 3 92
Lesson 4 94
Lesson 5 96
Lesson 6 98
Lesson 7 100
Lesson 8 102
Writing Roundup 104

unit 6
Inference

What Is an Inference? 106
Practice Making Inferences 107
Lesson 1 108
Lesson 2 110
Lesson 3 112
Lesson 4 114
Lesson 5 116
Lesson 6 118
Lesson 7 120
Lesson 8 122
Writing Roundup 124

Check Yourself 126

What Are Facts?

Facts are sometimes called details. They are small pieces of information. Facts can appear in true stories, such as those in the newspaper. Facts can also appear in legends and other stories that people make up.

How to Read for Facts

You can find facts by asking yourself questions. Ask *who*, and your answer will be a fact about a person. Ask *what*, and your answer will be a fact about a thing. Ask *where*, and your answer will be a fact about a place. Ask *when*, and your answer will be a fact about a time. Ask *how many* or *how much*, and your answer will be a fact about a number or an amount.

Try It!

Read this story and look for facts as you read. Ask yourself *how many* and *what*.

Snakes

If you're afraid of snakes, maybe it's because you don't know much about these interesting animals. There are more than 2,400 different kinds of snakes. They live on every continent of the world except Antarctica. They come in all sizes. The largest snake ever measured was a python that was 32 feet long. One of the smallest is the thread snake, which is only about 4 inches long.

Did you find these facts when you read the paragraph? Write the facts on the lines below.

◆ How many different kinds of snakes are there?

Fact: _____

◆ What is one of the smallest snakes?

Fact: _____

Practice Finding Facts

Below are some practice questions. The first two are already answered. Answer the third one on your own.

___B___ **1.** The thread snake is
- **A.** 4 feet long
- **B.** 4 inches long
- **C.** 32 feet long
- **D.** 32 inches long

Look at the question and answers again. The word *long* is asking for a number. There are many numbers in the paragraph, but you are looking for one that describes the length of the thread snake. Read the paragraph until you find the words *thread snake*. You should find this sentence: "One of the smallest is the thread snake, which is only about 4 inches long." Anwer **B** is the correct answer. Answer **C** is also a fact from the story, but it describes pythons, not thread snakes.

___C___ **2.** The continent that has no snakes is
- **A.** Africa
- **B.** Australia
- **C.** Antarctica
- **D.** America

Look at the question. It asks for the name of a *continent* that has no snakes. Search the story about snakes for the name of a continent. You should find this sentence: "They live on every continent of the world except Antarctica." The words are a little different from the words in the story. The words "except Antarctica" tell you that Antarctica has no snakes, so the answer is **C**.

Now it's your turn to practice. Answer the next question by writing the letter of the correct answer on the line.

_____ **3.** The largest snake ever measured was
- **A.** a python
- **B.** a continent snake
- **C.** a thread snake
- **D.** an Antarctic snake

Read each story. After each story you will answer questions about the facts in the story. Remember, a fact is something that you know is true.

Hug Someone Else, Please!

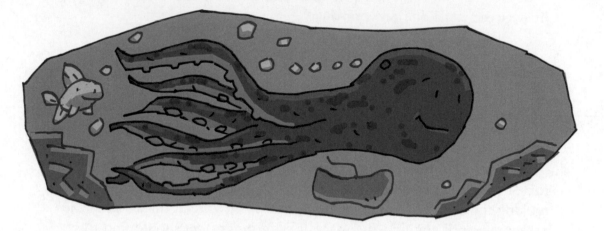

Many people think that an octopus makes a curious sight. It has eight arms coming out of a rounded head. Its name, *octopus*, comes from two Greek words that mean "eight feet."

People once thought that the octopus was a "devilfish" or a "monster of the sea." They thought that an octopus had arms long enough to hug a whole ship. Experts today know that this is not true. These odd sea creatures actually prefer to be left alone. Even the largest type of octopus is too small to hug a ship. Their average length is only about 10 feet. Most kinds of octopus are not any larger than a person's fist. However, an octopus that feels threatened *will* bite, using its sharp, parrotlike beak. Also, every once in a while, an octopus will "hug" a diver.

_____ 1. An octopus has
    A. six arms   **C.** eight arms
    B. four arms   **D.** two arms

_____ 2. People once thought that the octopus was a
    A. mammal   **C.** whale
    B. monster   **D.** pet

_____ 3. The octopus likes to
    A. be left alone   **C.** attack people
    B. play with people   **D.** swim beside boats

_____ 4. The average length of an octopus is
    A. 12 feet   **C.** 10 feet
    B. 30 feet   **D.** 50 feet

_____ 5. Octopuses have parrotlike
    A. wings   **C.** eyes
    B. beaks   **D.** tails

Even though it cannot pull ships down into the sea, an octopus can use its arms to move rocks much heavier than itself. Its arms can also handle tiny objects quite well. In one study scientists placed food for an octopus in screw-top jars. The octopus unscrewed the lid and then ate the food from the jar.

An octopus uses its arms mainly to gather food. It eats shellfish, including clams, crabs, and lobsters. It leaves its den at the bottom of the sea at night. When an octopus finds a crab or something else good to eat, it releases poison into the water. This makes the victim easy to catch. For the trip home, the octopus gathers the food into the skin between its arms. This area is called the web. When its web is full, the octopus returns home for a fine meal.

_____ **6.** An octopus will use its arms to
      A. sink ships   **C.** poison a crab
      B. attack people   **D.** move large objects

_____ **7.** When given a screw-top jar, an octopus will probably
      A. break it   **C.** swallow it
      B. open it   **D.** look at it

_____ **8.** An octopus uses its arms mainly to
      A. eat   **C.** move rocks
      B. fight   **D.** carry young

_____ **9.** The octopus carries its food in
      A. its mouth   **C.** a layer of skin
      B. its beak   **D.** its gills

_____ **10.** The octopus eats its meals
      A. above its den   **C.** away from home
      B. in its den   **D.** while swimming

Cats in History

Cats first became pets long, long ago. This may have happened as early as 3500 B.C. People in early Egypt loved cats. The cats kept homes free of rats, mice, and snakes. Cats also kept pests away from farms and places where grain was stored.

A thousand years later, cats in Egypt had become more important than ever. They were protected by law. Under the law, people who harmed cats could be put to death. Also during this time, cat owners had a special way to express their sadness when a pet cat died. The owners shaved their eyebrows to show how much they had loved their special pet. Cats even became part of the religion in certain areas of Egypt. In those places people prayed to a goddess of love named Bast. Statues of Bast had a cat's head and a woman's body.

_____ **1.** Cats became pets as early as
   A. 1000 B.C.   **C.** 3500 B.C.
   B. 2000 B.C.   **D.** 5000 B.C.

_____ **2.** Cats in early Egypt kept pests away from
   A. farms   **C.** streets
   B. rats   **D.** trees

_____ **3.** People who harmed cats were sometimes
   A. put in jail   **C.** given honors
   B. cheered   **D.** put to death

_____ **4.** When cats died, their owners shaved their
   A. heads   **C.** arms
   B. eyebrows   **D.** beards

_____ **5.** Bast had a cat's
   A. legs   **C.** body
   B. fur   **D.** head

People in the Far East also loved cats. They used cats to keep mice from nibbling holy books in temples. Cats also kept mice from eating silkworm cocoons. Silk makers traded silk cloth for other fine goods, so they depended on their cats.

Cats in Europe in the 1300s were not treated as well. People killed them by the thousands because they were a symbol of bad luck. This caused the number of rats to grow. Rats carried diseases. A deadly disease called the Black Death spread, killing one-fourth of all people in Europe.

Over time people once again learned that cats keep many pests away. By the 1600s cats had again become popular. Settlers arriving in the New World brought cats with them. Some of the cats you know today came from those early cats.

_____ **6.** Cats in the Far East kept mice away from
      A. water   **C.** cocoons
      B. people   **D.** Europe

_____ **7.** People in Europe in the 1300s thought cats were
      A. cute   **C.** good
      B. fun   **D.** bad

_____ **8.** With fewer cats the number of rats
      A. was larger   **C.** stayed the same
      B. was smaller   **D.** was unimportant

_____ **9.** One-fourth of the people in Europe
      A. moved   **C.** owned cats
      B. died   **D.** loved cats

_____ **10.** By the 1600s people once again
      A. liked cats   **C.** killed cats
      B. saved rats   **D.** hated cats

Steeplejacks

Do you know what a steeplejack is? First you have to know what a steeple is. A steeple is a tower on a church. A steeplejack is someone who repairs steeples. Steeplejacks may also do painting or cleaning.

There is a family of steeplejacks. They travel around the country finding work as they go. They carry a scrapbook showing the steeples they have repaired. In addition to churches, they work on courthouses and other buildings with towers.

Many of these buildings are old and in need of careful repair. The steeplejacks climb up to look. Often they work with engineers and other experts to decide what to do. Then the family goes to work. Some jobs take a few weeks. Other jobs take months.

_____ **1.** A steeple is a church
    A. door   **C.** tower
    B. bell   **D.** window

_____ **2.** Steeplejacks do painting and
    A. watering   **C.** preaching
    B. waxing   **D.** cleaning

_____ **3.** Besides fixing churches, steeplejacks sometimes work on
    A. courthouses   **C.** courtyards
    B. churchyards   **D.** courtrooms

_____ **4.** The first step of a steeplejack's job is to
    A. work for weeks   **C.** paint the steeple
    B. look at problems   **D.** clean the steeple

_____ **5.** Steeplejacks often work with
    A. engines   **C.** trains
    B. reporters   **D.** engineers

Many steeples have lovely clocks on them. Sometimes the golden numbers on the clocks have worn out. The steeplejacks replace the worn-out numbers and cover them with thin pieces of gold. Then the clock numbers shine just as they did in the past.

Some steeples have weather vanes on top that need repair. Sometimes the roof of a steeple is worn out. The steeplejacks repair the roofs too. If a steeple is made of metal, then parts of it may have rusted. The steeplejacks replace these parts. If a steeple is made of wood, it may need to be painted. Sometimes steeplejacks paint the inside of a steeple too.

Steeplejacks work in high places and do a lot of climbing. They have to be careful. They don't work in the rain, and they stay home on windy days.

_____ **6.** Sometimes steeplejacks have to replace clock
     A. hands   **C.** alarms
     B. times   **D.** numbers

_____ **7.** Weather vanes on steeples sometimes have to be
     A. turned   **C.** repaired
     B. blown   **D.** finished

_____ **8.** Sometimes steeplejacks repair
     A. roofs   **C.** watches
     B. ladders   **D.** bricks

_____ **9.** Steeplejacks do not work in the
     A. winter   **C.** steeples
     B. clocks   **D.** wind

_____ **10.** In their work steeplejacks need to be very
     A. careful   **C.** careless
     B. stormy   **D.** windy

Please Pass the Drink Fruit

Chimpanzees do not have speech organs that allow them to speak. They can make noises, but they cannot say words. They do have hands with four fingers and a thumb, so some chimps have been able to learn Ameslan, American Sign Language. This is the sign language used by some people who are deaf.

One of the first chimps to learn Ameslan was Washoe. Born in 1965, Washoe began learning to sign words when she was one year old. Like many toddlers, the first "word" she learned was *more*. When she was six, she could use more than 200 signs. Washoe's teachers, Allen and Beatrice Gardner, treated Washoe as their own child. She lived with them in their home, and she did not see other chimpanzees. When she did meet another chimp, she must have thought that it was a strange creature. Her sign for chimp was *bug*.

_____ 1. Chimpanzees do not have
   A. a tongue   C. speech organs
   B. a throat   D. teeth

_____ 2. A sign language used by some deaf people is called
   A. English   C. Washoe
   B. Ameslan   D. Gardner

_____ 3. Washoe's first "word" was
   A. go   C. drink
   B. bug   D. more

_____ 4. When she was six, Washoe could use more than
   A. 200 signs   C. 300 signs
   B. 250 signs   D. 1,000 signs

_____ 5. Washoe probably thought that other chimps were
   A. her teachers   C. strange creatures
   B. her friends   D. deaf people

Lucy is another chimpanzee that learned sign language. She was born a year after Washoe and lived with another family, the Temerlins. The Temerlins taught her to sign, and she learned quickly. She learned to ask for one of her favorite foods by signing the words for *candy drink fruit*. When Lucy did this, the Temerlins knew that she wanted watermelon. Washoe also made up a word for watermelon. She called it *drink fruit* too.

The Temerlins and the Gardners have found that Lucy and Washoe are like humans in many ways. Sometimes they behave as if they are human. When they are joyful, they clap their hands. When they are angry, they sometimes call their enemies names. They use names they have learned in sign language.

_____ **6.** Lucy was a good
     A. student   **C.** musician
     B. athlete   **D.** teacher

_____ **7.** Both Lucy and Washoe made up a word for
     A. drink   **C.** watermelon
     B. fruit   **D.** candy

_____ **8.** In many ways chimps are like
     A. bugs   **C.** names
     B. people   **D.** their enemies

_____ **9.** When a chimp claps its hands, it is probably
     A. angry   **C.** happy
     B. sad   **D.** thinking

_____ **10.** When a chimp is angry, it might
     A. bite   **C.** call others names
     B. swing its arms   **D.** jump up and down

Sluggers at Work

The wood for baseball bats comes from the ash-tree forests of Pennsylvania. Ash wood is especially strong, so it makes good baseball bats. Ash trees are thin compared to other trees. In a high wind, an ash tree can break and fall. However, in the Pennsylvania forests, thicker kinds of trees grow all around the ash trees. These thick trees keep the ash trees from bending too far in a wind storm.

At Slugger Park workers make baseball bats out of ash trees. Workers and their machines can make an ordinary bat in about eight seconds. It takes longer to make a bat for a major-league player. Many of these players want bats that meet their special needs. Once Ted Williams, a famous baseball player, returned some bats to Slugger Park. "The grips just don't feel right to me," he said. The workers carefully measured the grips. Sure enough, Williams was right! The grips were wrong by just a small fraction of an inch.

_____ **1.** Wooden baseball bats are made
    A. in wind storms   **C.** from ash trees
    B. in forests   **D.** from thick trees

_____ **2.** Thick trees protect ash trees from
    A. breaking   **C.** playing
    B. growing   **D.** cutting

_____ **3.** Workers can make an ordinary bat in about
    A. ten seconds   **C.** twelve seconds
    B. thirty seconds   **D.** eight seconds

_____ **4.** Many major-league players want bats that are
    A. special   **C.** stronger
    B. returned   **D.** longer

_____ **5.** When Ted Williams didn't like the grips, he
    A. gave the bats away   **C.** measured the grips
    B. sent the bats back   **D.** used the bats anyway

Some players use many bats in a single game. Orlando Cepeda used to throw away a bat after he made a hit with it. He thought that each bat had only a certain number of hits in it. No one could tell how many hits were in a bat. Maybe there was only one. "So why take a chance?" asked Cepeda. When it was his turn to face the pitcher again, he grabbed a brand new Slugger Park bat.

The Slugger Park factory also makes aluminum bats. These are used mostly by college teams and minor-league players. Aluminum bats last longer than wooden ones do. Many baseball fans hope that major-league players will never use these new bats, however. When you hit a ball with one, the sound you hear is a soft *ping*. Fans like to hear the solid *crack* made by a strong wooden bat. Baseball fans don't like the game to change.

_____ **6.** Some players use many bats
      A. over and over   **C.** in a single game
      B. for their fans   **D.** at the same time

_____ **7.** Orlando Cepeda threw away a bat after he
      A. made a hit   **C.** faced the pitcher
      B. took a chance   **D.** had an idea

_____ **8.** Some college teams use
      A. oak bats   **C.** 15 bats
      B. aluminum bats   **D.** fans

_____ **9.** Many baseball fans don't like
      A. college teams   **C.** aluminum bats
      B. pitchers   **D.** major-league players

_____ **10.** Compared to wooden bats, aluminum bats
      A. feel better   **C.** miss balls
      B. break often   **D.** last longer

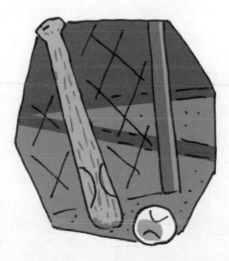

The Midnight Tulip

It was after midnight. A Dutch farmer made one last trip through his greenhouse before going to bed. He walked past rows and rows of tulips. Suddenly he stopped. There, blooming in the early morning hours, was a rare flower. It was a black tulip. In the morning the excited farmer took the tulip to a flower show. By evening the farmer and his prize plant were on television. He was a hero.

Most tulips are red, yellow, white, or pink. A black tulip takes years to develop. The farmer worked on his midnight tulip for seven years. He crossed two dark-purple tulips. They made a seed. The seed took years to grow into a round bulb. Finally a black flower grew from the bulb.

Tulips are a major industry for the Dutch people. Tulip sales bring in millions of dollars.

_____ 1. The farmer made one last trip through his
  A. grayhouse   **C.** bath house
  B. greenhouse   **D.** pumphouse

_____ 2. The midnight tulip was
  A. dry   **C.** rare
  B. red   **D.** late

_____ 3. The farmer crossed tulips that were
  A. pink   **C.** white
  B. black   **D.** purple

_____ 4. Tulip flowers grow from
  A. leaves   **C.** roots
  B. bulbs   **D.** greenhouses

_____ 5. For the Dutch people, tulips are a major
  A. import   **C.** industry
  B. million   **D.** problem

The Dutch people first received tulips in the early 1600s. The tulips came from the Far East. The Dutch loved the beautiful flowers, and soon grew their own.

People began trying to produce new kinds of tulips. The results were striped tulips, double tulips, and lily tulips. People grew tulips of many new colors, but black tulips were very rare. Someone grew a black tulip in 1891. Another black tulip bloomed in 1955. It was called Queen of the Night.

Now black tulips grow in ordinary gardens. The Dutch farmer is working on two other unusual tulips. He hopes to grow a tulip that is dark blue. He wants to grow bright green tulips, too. It may take 20 years before they can be sold.

_____ **6.** Tulips were brought to the Dutch people in
       A. 1891   **C.** the 1500s
       B. 1955   **D.** the 1600s

_____ **7.** Tulips first came from
       A. the Far East   **C.** farmers
       B. the Dutch   **D.** queens

_____ **8.** Black tulips bloomed in 1891 and in
       A. 1981   **C.** 1595
       B. 1955   **D.** 1819

_____ **9.** Developing bulbs to sell takes
       A. 16 years   **C.** ordinary gardens
       B. 20 years   **D.** double blooms

_____ **10.** The farmer is working on two other tulips that will be
       A. double   **C.** ordinary
       B. different   **D.** striped

Money Doctors

Have you ever ripped a dollar bill by mistake? If so, perhaps you taped it back together. Sometimes money is damaged in more serious ways. Then it is not as easy to fix. If you cannot repair paper money, you cannot use it. You have to send badly damaged money to a special government office in Washington, D.C.

The people who work in this office sit at long tables under bright lights. Their main tools are magnifying glasses and tweezers. Their job is to piece together the damaged bills. The workers try to find at least half of each bill. Otherwise the government will not pay the owner for it.

This office is very busy. It handles about 30,000 cases per year. People may wait a long time before their case comes up, but it's worth it. The service is free, and you may get your money back.

_____ **1.** If you cannot repair paper money, you cannot
    A. buy it   **C.** hide it
    B. use it   **D.** send it

_____ **2.** You can send badly damaged money to a government
    A. bank   **C.** office
    B. bill   **D.** tool

_____ **3.** The workers' main tools are magnifying glasses and
    A. tables   **C.** tweezers
    B. tape   **D.** lights

_____ **4.** Workers find half of a bill so the government will
    A. pay the owner   **C.** call the owner
    B. fix the money   **D.** take the job

_____ **5.** The services of this office are
    A. expensive   **C.** early
    B. free   **D.** easy

How is money damaged? Sometimes it is damaged in a fire. Then a person may have mostly ashes to send in. Sometimes money is damaged in a flood. Then the bills are faded and stuck together. People have sent money that had gone through the washing machine. Some bills have been chewed by animals. Others somehow got into blenders.

Also some people don't like banks, so they hide their money in unusual places. If bills are buried in cans, they sometimes get moldy. Mice often nibble at money hidden in attics and basements.

Once, a truck carrying money for a bank exploded. There was a big fire. The truck company sent in the remains of the bills. They were worth $2.5 million dollars. Thanks to the government workers, the company got a check for all the money.

_____ **6.** When bills are burned, they turn to
        A. coins   **C.** dust
        B. ashes   **D.** sand

_____ **7.** When bills get wet, they
        A. fade   **C.** fall
        B. burn   **D.** blend

_____ **8.** Some people hide money because they don't like
        A. fires   **C.** mice
        B. checks   **D.** banks

_____ **9.** One time, money carried in a truck was burned in
        A. lightning   **C.** an explosion
        B. a basement   **D.** an airplane

_____**10.** Thanks to the workers, the company was able to
        A. put out the fire   **C.** get the money back
        B. write a check   **D.** buy the money back

A Life of Art

Frida Kahlo was a famous Mexican painter. Many claim that she is Mexico's greatest artist. As a child she dreamed of becoming a doctor, but a traffic accident changed her entire life. At age 15 Kahlo was riding on a bus in Mexico City. It crashed into a trolley car. Kahlo was seriously hurt and had to stay in the hospital a long time. She felt her dreams of being a doctor were over.

In the hospital Kahlo grew bored. She began to paint to fill her time. She once had taken art lessons from a teacher who thought she had great talent. Kahlo now hoped she could make a living by selling her paintings.

_____ **1.** Frida Kahlo was a famous Mexican
   A. painter   **C.** writer
   B. doctor   **D.** singer

_____ **2.** Kahlo's life was changed by a
   A. new teacher   **C.** total stranger
   B. traffic accident **D.** family doctor

_____ **3.** Kahlo had once dreamed of being
   A. an artist   **C.** a doctor
   B. an author   **D.** a teacher

_____ **4.** In the hospital Kahlo
   A. knitted scarves **C.** wrote many letters
   B. began to paint   **D.** grew much sicker

_____ **5.** A former teacher thought Kahlo
   A. needed classes   **C.** had great talent
   B. had little talent **D.** should work for him

Most of Kahlo's works were self-portraits. She used bold and harsh colors. They showed the pain that she felt in her body. People praised the art for being so original. Many of her works show symbols from Mexican history as well. She also liked to paint herself in native clothing and jewelry.

At age 22 Kahlo wed Diego Rivera. He was an artist best known for his murals. Many of Kahlo's new paintings showed her feelings about marriage and children.

Sadly, Kahlo's pain never left her. She had 35 operations in her lifetime. Yet she produced many works of art that people still greatly admire.

_____ **6.** Most of Kahlo's paintings were
       A. about buses   **C.** about her husband
       B. done in watercolors   **D.** of herself

_____ **7.** Kahlo's art reflected her
       A. sense of direction   **C.** own feelings
       B. sense of shame   **D.** youth

_____ **8.** Kahlo often painted herself in
       A. dark outfits   **C.** modern jewelry
       B. large hats   **D.** native clothing

_____ **9.** Diego Rivera was Kahlo's
       A. husband   **C.** doctor
       B. art teacher   **D.** neighbor

_____ **10.** People praised Kahlo's art for
       A. being humorous   **C.** its pale colors
       B. being so original   **D.** its high cost

Writing Roundup

Read the story below. Think about the facts. Then answer the questions in complete sentences.

Salt has always been considered a valuable item. In ancient times it was often traded ounce for ounce with gold. In China people once used coins made of salt. In other countries workers were paid with salt cakes or bags of salt. You may have heard the expression, "You are worth your salt." It means you are worth the money you are being paid.

All salt comes from water in seas and lakes. The salty water is called brine. Some salt is also found underground, but even that salt came from sea water that evaporated over time.

1. What was salt often traded for in ancient times?

_____

_____

2. What does the saying "You are worth your salt" mean?

_____

_____

3. What is salty water called?

_____

_____

Prewriting

Think of an idea you might write about, such as a product you use or an important invention. Write the idea in the center of the idea web below. Then fill out the rest of the web with facts.

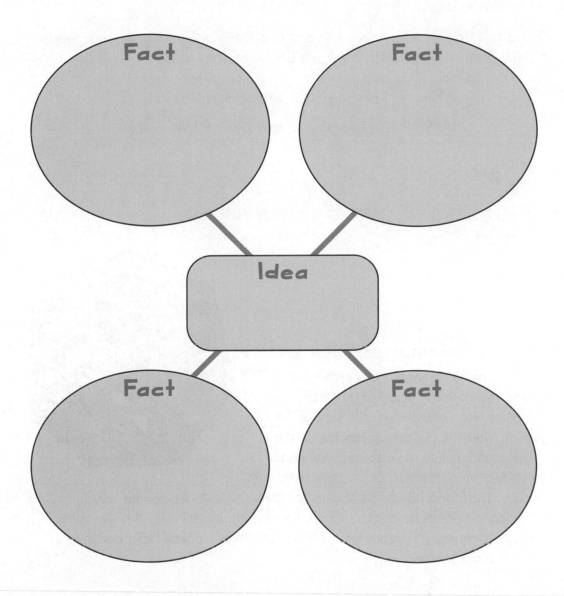

On Your Own

Now use another sheet of paper to write a paragraph about your idea. Use the facts from your idea web.

What Is Sequence?

Sequence means time order, or 1-2-3 order. If several things happen in a story, they happen in a sequence. One event happens first, and it is followed by another event.

You can find the sequence of events in a story by looking for time words, such as *first*, *next*, and *last*. Here is a list of time words:

later	during	days of the week
today	while	months of the year

Try It!

This paragraph tells a story. Try to follow the sequence. Circle all the time words.

George Washington Carver

George Washington Carver was a famous American scientist. He was born in Missouri. Later he went to school in Iowa. Then he became a teacher at the Tuskegee Institute in Alabama. While he was teaching, he also did experiments with crops. He found hundreds of uses for peanuts, sweet potatoes, and soybeans. When he died in 1943, he was known all over the world for his discoveries. Ten years later, the home where he was born became a national monument.

Try putting these events in the order that they happened. What happened first? Write the number **1** on the line by that sentence. Then write the number **2** by the sentence that tells what happened next. Write the number **3** by the sentence that tells what happened last.

_____ Carver made many discoveries.

_____ Carver's home became a national monument.

_____ Carver became a teacher at the Tuskegee Institute.

Practice with Sequence

Here are some practice sequence questions. The first two are already answered. You can do the third one on your own.

___C___ **1.** When did Carver do experiments with crops?
      A. before he was in Missouri
      B. after he became famous
      C. while he was teaching

The question has the words, "experiments with crops." Find those words in the story about Carver. You will find them in the sentence, "While he was teaching, he also did experiments with crops." Find the time word in that sentence. The word is *while*. The words, "while he was teaching" are the same as answer **C**, so **C** is correct.

___B___ **2.** Where did Carver go just before he went to Alabama?
      A. Missouri
      B. Iowa
      C. Tuskegee

Look at the question carefully. Notice the time word *before*. Notice also that the word *just* is there. The question is asking where Carver went *just before* he went to Alabama. In the story you will find these sentences: "He was born in Missouri. Later he went to school in Iowa. Then he became a teacher at the Tuskegee Institute in Alabama." Answer **B** is correct. Answer **A** tells where he was born, but not where he was *just before* he went to Alabama. Answer **C** is not correct because it is the name of the place where he went in Alabama.

_____ **3.** When did Carver's home become a national monument?
      A. when he lived in Alabama
      B. after he died
      C. while he was teaching

Read each story. After each story you will answer questions about the sequence of events in the story. Remember, sequence is the order of things.

Remarkable Journey

How does a young dog or cat get to know a new home? The animal uses its nose. Right away it sniffs its new surroundings. Then it makes wider and wider circles, sniffing all the time. Before long it can find its way home very well, even in the dark. It simply follows familiar scents.

Stories exist of animals who found their way across land they had never sniffed before. Take the case of Smoky, the Persian cat. Smoky had a funny tuft of red fur under his chin. One day Smoky and his owner began a long journey. They were moving from Oklahoma to Tennessee. When they were just 18 miles from their Oklahoma home, Smoky jumped out of the car. Somehow he found his way back to the old house. There he wandered around outside for many days. Finally he disappeared.

A year later Smoky meowed at the door of a house in Tennessee. A man opened the door. "Is that you, Smoky?" he whispered. At first he couldn't believe it. Then he recognized the tuft of red fur. It was Smoky!

A dog named Bobby also made a remarkable journey. Bobby lived at a farmhouse in a small town in France. One day Bobby's master decided to take him to Paris, which was 35 miles away. For hours the two wandered through the crowded, noisy city. At the end of the day, when it was time to go home, Bobby's master looked down. The dog had disappeared! The man searched everywhere, but he finally decided that his dog was gone forever, and he sadly went home. Five days later Bobby was barking at the farmhouse door!

Perhaps the most amazing journey of all was made by Prince, a dog who belonged to a British soldier. During World War I, Prince's master was sent to France to fight. After his master left, Prince somehow crossed a wide body of water called the English Channel. Remarkably the dog managed to find his master in the trench where he was fighting.

1. Put these events in the order that they happened. What happened first? Write the number **1** on the line by that sentence. Then write the number **2** by the sentence that tells what happened next. Write the number **3** by the sentence that tells what happened last.

_____ Smoky traveled to Tennessee.

_____ Smoky jumped out of the car.

_____ Smoky went to his old home.

_____ **2.** What is the first thing a pet does in a new place?
   A. travels long distances
   B. explores its surroundings
   C. finds its way in the dark

_____ **3.** When was the man sure the cat was Smoky?
   A. when he saw the tuft of fur
   B. as soon as he opened the door
   C. before he opened the door

_____ **4.** When did the man discover that Bobby was gone?
   A. after 35 miles
   B. five days later
   C. at the end of the day

_____ **5.** What did Prince do just before he found his master?
   A. found the British Army
   B. crossed the English Channel
   C. located a trench

Meat-Eating Plants

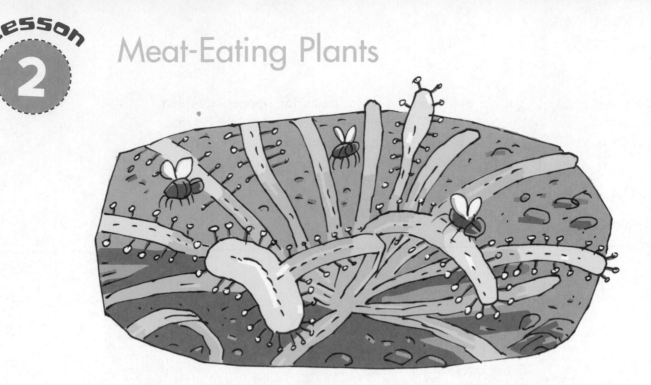

Sundews are beautiful little plants. They seem so small and harmless. All around the edges of their leaves are tiny hairs that glisten with a shiny liquid. To an insect this liquid looks like food. The insect lands on the leaf. The liquid is sticky, and the insect cannot get loose. The sundew wraps itself around the insect and eats it.

Many years ago a scientist named Charles Darwin became fascinated with sundews. Would they eat only insects? Darwin put small bits of roast lamb on the sticky leaves. The plant gobbled them up. Darwin next tried drops of milk, bits of egg, and other foods. The sundew loved them all.

Sundews are just one kind of *meat-eating* plant. These plants trap insects in different ways. Some, like the sundew, use their tiny hairs. Others, like the pitcher plant, have bright colors that attract insects. When an insect lands on the colorful petals, the bug starts falling. The insect slides down into the slippery insides of the plant. At the bottom is a pool of liquid. Special chemicals in this liquid turn the insect into food for the flower.

Bladderworts are meat-eating plants that live mostly in water. Bladderworts have trapdoors in their sides. When an insect comes near the tiny hairs on a bladderwort leaf, the trapdoor opens. The insect is pulled inside.

Some plants collect rainwater at their base. When insects go to get the water, they cannot escape. The plants are lined with a powder that makes it impossible for the insects to get away. A scientist named Durland Fish put four of the plants on a fence around a garden. Within eight days these four plants trapped 136 insects.

1. Put these events in the order that they happened. What happened first? Write the number **1** on the line by that sentence. Then write the number **2** by the sentence that tells what happened next. Write the number **3** by the sentence that tells what happened last.

_____ An insect lands on a sundew leaf.

_____ The sundew wraps itself around the bug.

_____ The sundew's hairs glisten.

_____ **2.** When did Darwin become fascinated with sundews?
   A. recently
   B. years ago
   C. within eight days

_____ **3.** What did Darwin feed the plant before he fed it milk?
   A. roast lamb
   B. bits of egg
   C. a drinking straw

_____ **4.** When does the insect slide down into the pitcher plant?
   A. after the insect falls into a pool of liquid
   B. before the plant uses its hairs
   C. after the insect lands on the petals

_____ **5.** When does the bladderwort's trapdoor open?
   A. after the insect is pulled inside
   B. after the insect climbs out
   C. after the insect comes near its hairs

Giraffes

Giraffes are the tallest living animals. Most adult giraffes are tall enough to look into second-story windows. Their long necks help them get leaves and fruit that no other animal can reach. Let's see how a giraffe's life begins.

A female giraffe, or cow, gives birth to a baby 15 months after mating. The mother searches for a safe place to give birth. Both the baby, or calf, and the mother are in a great deal of danger right after the birth. More than half of all baby giraffes are killed by lions, cheetahs, or hyenas minutes after birth.

With a thud, the new baby drops the 5 feet from its mother to the ground. It weighs about 130 pounds and is 6 feet tall. The baby can run and jump 10 hours after it is born, but it cannot outrun an enemy.

The mother hides the calf in tall grass. Then she goes to search for food. The baby is fairly safe as long as it stays still. The cow returns to nurse the baby. The calf stays hidden for about a month.

After a month the mother and baby join a group of four or five other cows with their calves. The calves stay together while their mothers gather food. Sometimes one mother stays with them. The cows return at night to protect the calves. The calves stay in this group until they are about a year old.

By the time they are a year old, the giraffes from 10 to 12 feet tall. They can outrun all of their enemies except the cheetah. A cheetah rarely attacks an animal larger than itself. Giraffes continue to grow until they are seven or eight years old. Adults are between 14 and 18 feet tall.

1. Put these events in the order that they happened. What happened first? Write the number **1** on the line by that sentence. Then write the number **2** by the sentence that tells what happened next. Write the number **3** by the sentence that tells what happened last.

_____ The baby can run and jump.

_____ The baby drops 5 feet to the ground.

_____ The female giraffe looks for a safe place to give birth.

_____ **2.** When does a female giraffe give birth?
   A. after she joins a group of other cows
   B. every year
   C. 15 months after mating

_____ **3.** When are the mother and baby in danger?
   A. 10 hours after the baby's birth
   B. right after the baby's birth
   C. 15 months after the baby's birth

_____ **4.** When do the cow and calf join a group of other females and babies?
   A. about a month after the baby is born
   B. when the calf is a year old
   C. when the calf is seven or eight years old

_____ **5.** When do giraffes stop growing?
   A. when they are
      three or four years old
   B. when they are
      seven or eight years old
   C. when they join a
      group of other giraffes

Telltale Prints

Eyewitnesses say Louie stole a necklace. Officer Valdez needs more evidence. She recalls fingerprinting Louie and his brother when they got in trouble last year. If prints at this crime scene are the same as the ones on file, she's got a strong case.

Officer Valdez sprinkles colored powder on a book, jewelry box, shelf, phone, and doorknob. She puts a chemical on cloth items. These treatments show the finger marks left by natural oil from skin. Photos are taken. At the police station, she looks in the computer file for a match. The prints match someone else. The thief was Louie's identical twin, Lester!

This tale shows how fingerprints can be used. In the 1880s, Sir Francis Galton did studies in Great Britain that proved no two people have the same prints. Ten years later, Sir Edward R. Henry made a system to recognize criminals by their prints. Other countries used it. In 1924, the United States set up a print file at the FBI. It has cards with prints of more than 173 million people.

A print is the pattern of ridges on the pad of a finger. These last a lifetime unless they are altered by disease or injury. When Officer Valdez made Louie's prints, she first pressed his finger pad in ink. Then she rolled it on a card from side to side. This was repeated for each finger.

You can create your own prints. Scribble with a pencil on a piece of paper until you have a gray smudge. Rub your finger pad in the smudge. Press a piece of clear tape on your finger. Stick the tape to a card. There's your fingerprint!

1. Put these events in the order that they happened. What happened first? Write the number **1** on the line by that sentence. Then write the number **2** by the sentence that tells what happened next. Write the number **3** by the sentence that tells what happened last.

_____ The United States set up a fingerprint file at the FBI.

_____ Sir Edward Henry set up a system to recognize criminals.

_____ Sir Francis Galton proved people have different prints.

_____ **2.** What was the first thing Officer Valdez did to find fingerprints at the scene of the crime?
   A. sprinkled colored powder on a doorknob
   B. looked in the computer files
   C. put on her glasses

_____ **3.** When was a system made to recognize criminals by their prints?
   A. in the 1920s
   B. in the 1880s
   C. in the 1890s

_____ **4.** What did Officer Valdez do after she pressed Louie's finger in ink?
   A. put a chemical on cloth items
   B. scribbled with a pencil
   C. rolled it on a card

_____ **5.** To take your own fingerprint, when do you put tape on your finger?
   A. before you scribble a pencil smudge
   B. before you press it in ink
   C. after you rub your finger in the smudge

Changes in Farming

What job would you have had if you had lived in England in 1540? Chances are you would have been a farmer. Most people were. It took many people to raise enough food. Now just two out of 100 people in England farm. The rest work in towns and cities. This pattern is true in many parts of the world. What allowed so many people to leave the farm?

Several discoveries and inventions caused this change. One of these was rotating, or changing, crops. Farmers had long known that growing the same crop in the same field year after year made the soil poor. For this reason they usually left fields empty part of the time.

In the early 1700s, Charles Townshend found a way to rotate four crops. This way fields could be used all year. For example, four fields would be planted with wheat, clover, barley, and turnips. By rotating the crop grown in each field every year, the soil remained rich. Grasslands that could not be used before could now be farmed. This rotation system allowed farmers to raise much more food, both for themselves and their animals.

Robert Bakewell was an English farmer in the late 1700s. He wanted to raise better farm animals. He produced better horses, cattle, and sheep. He developed a sheep that could be raised for meat as well as for wool.

The invention of new farm tools also led to great change. Around 1700, the seed drill was invented. Before that time seeds were scattered by hand. The seed drill dug trenches in the dirt and planted the seeds. This tool was the first modern farm machine. Crop rotation, better farm animals, and new farm tools made it possible for fewer people to produce a lot of food. Thousands of families moved from farms to the cities.

1. Put these events in the order that they happened. What happened first? Write the number **1** on the line by that sentence. Then write the number **2** by the sentence that tells what happened next. Write the number **3** by the sentence that tells what happened last.

_____ Townshend developed a system of crop rotation.

_____ The seed drill was invented.

_____ Thousand of families moved to cities.

_____ **2.** When were most people farmers?
    A. in the 1980s
    B. after the invention of the seed drill
    C. before the 1700s

_____ **3.** When were seeds scattered by hand?
    A. during the 1900s
    B. before the seed drill was invented
    C. during the winter

_____ **4.** When were better farm animals developed?
    A. during the late 1700s
    B. before Townshend lived
    C. after people moved to the cities

_____ **5.** When was the seed drill invented?
    A. in 1540
    B. after crop rotation was developed
    C. before Bakewell produced better animals

Yellowstone Park on Fire!

The year 1988 will not be forgotten for a long time at Yellowstone National Park. Fires broke out in June and burned fiercely until September. The flames were not put out completely until November. They covered almost half of the huge park. What caused such huge fires? There are several answers to this question.

Lodgepole pines make up 80 percent of the park's forests. These trees grow quickly, but they only live about 200 years. Then many of the pines die and are blown down by high winds. The trees lie on the forest floor for many years. In wet forests they would rot and turn back into soil, but it is too dry for this to happen in Yellowstone. In 1988, dead wood covered the forest floor.

Yellowstone usually gets a lot of snow in the winter. When the snow melts, it provides water for the plants. For six winters in the 1980s, little snow had fallen. Rain also usually falls during the summer months, but 1988 was the driest summer in 116 years.

Several fires started in and near the park in June. Park officials fought the fires caused by human carelessness. They didn't try to put out the fires started by lightning. They knew that fires help clean out the dead wood. When little rain fell in June and July, the fires became larger and larger. More than 17,000 acres had burned by July 21. Park officials decided that it was time to fight all of the roaring fires.

On June 23, strong winds blew the fires into new areas of the park. Firefighters battled the blazes, but they had little success. On August 20, 80 mile-per-hour winds swept through the park. This day became known as Black Saturday. Fires that had almost died out came back to life. No matter how hard the firefighters tried, they couldn't control the flames. Snow and rain began to fall in September. Then the worst of the fires were put out. The remaining fires were put out by heavy snows in November.

1. Put these events in the order that they happened. What happened first? Write the number **1** on the line by that sentence. Then write the number **2** by the sentence that tells what happened next. Write the number **3** by the sentence that tells what happened last.

_____ Yellowstone had the driest summer in 116 years.

_____ The worst of the fires were put out.

_____ Several fires started in the park.

_____ **2.** When did the fires begin in Yellowstone?
    A. when the trees began to die
    B. when the heavy snows fell
    C. before the strong winds blew in

_____ **3.** When did little snow fall in the park?
    A. during the 1980s
    B. in November
    C. 116 years ago

_____ **4.** When did park officials decide to fight all of the fires?
    A. when lightning struck
    B. after 17,000 acres had burned
    C. on Black Saturday

_____ **5.** When was Black Saturday?
    A. when the trees died
    B. one month before the first fires started
    C. when strong winds hit the park

The History of Kites

No one knows when the first kite was made. The first record of a kite was more than 2,000 years ago in China. General Han Hsin was the leader of a rebel army. He wanted to overthrow a cruel king, but he had only a few men. Hsin decided to dig a tunnel into the king's castle. He flew a kite to determine how long the tunnel should be. The men in the tunnel took the kite string with them. When they reached the end of the string, they knew to dig up. They came up in the castle courtyard and defeated the king.

Kites have been flown in Japan for hundreds of years. In the 1700s, kites were flown in the fall to give thanks for a good harvest. Stalks of rice were tied to the kites. Kites were also flown to send good wishes to couples who had had their first son.

Today in Japan kites are often flown as part of a celebration, such as the beginning of a new year. The kites are painted to look like animals, heroes, and gods. Small kites as well as huge ones are made. Kite festivals are held each year in many regions of the country.

Kites have been used for scientific purposes in the western world. Most people have heard of Benjamin Franklin and his kite. Franklin had been studying electricity. He thought that lightning was a form of electricity, but he wasn't sure. In 1752, he tried to find out. He flew a kite in a storm. A key was attached to the kite. When sparks jumped from the key, it proved his idea was correct.

In the 1890s, Lawrence Hargrave invented the box kite. He used this kite to test ideas about flight. From 1898 until 1933, the United States Weather Bureau used box kites to gather weather data. The Wright Brothers also experimented with kites. What they learned helped them make the first airplane flight in 1903.

1. Put these events in the order that they happened. What happened first? Write the number **1** on the line by that sentence. Then write the number **2** by the sentence that tells what happened next. Write the number **3** by the sentence that tells what happened last.

_____ Franklin discovered that lightning was electricity.

_____ Han Hsin used a kite to measure distance.

_____ The Wright brothers experimented with kites.

_____ **2.** When was the first record of a kite?
   A. 100 years ago
   B. before Benjamin Franklin was born
   C. before General Han Hsin was born

_____ **3.** When were kites often flown in Japan?
   A. before a good harvest
   B. after the birth of a first son
   C. during storms

_____ **4.** When did Franklin fly a kite in a storm?
   A. before the cruel king was defeated
   B. before the Wrights experimented with kites
   C. when he studied electricity

_____ **5.** When did the Weather Bureau use kites?
   A. after the invention of the box kite
   B. before the Wright brothers made their first plane
   C. before Benjamin Franklin studied electricity

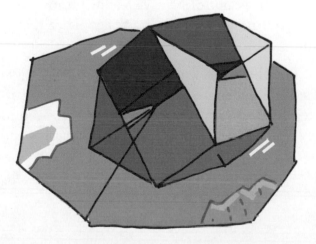

Dolphins

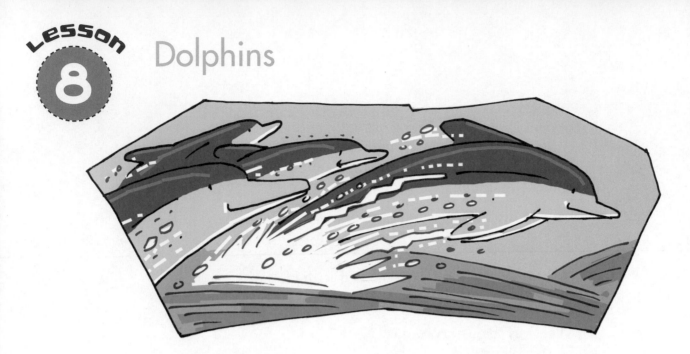

For centuries dolphins have been thought of as special animals. Plutarch, a Greek writer, praised their friendliness 2,000 years ago. Scenes of people riding on dolphins have appeared in the art of many countries.

There are more than 38 kinds of dolphins. Most types live in the ocean. They are related to whales. Dolphins are very smart. They can learn, remember, and solve problems. They are natural entertainers who love to perform. You can see them do tricks at marine amusement parks.

Dolphins travel in herds. They are social animals who like to play. They often toss seaweed and driftwood in the air. Dolphins become very unhappy and lonely if they are separated from their companions. Dolphins mate in the spring. A baby is born a year later. The other dolphins surround the mother while she is giving birth. They do this to protect her from danger. Soon after birth the mother pushes the baby to the surface so that it can breathe. The baby nurses, or drinks the mother's milk, for about 18 months. The mother teaches the baby and protects it from harm.

Many tales have been told of dolphins helping people. One famous dolphin was named Pelorus Jack. Jack lived in Cook's Strait between the North Island and the South Island of New Zealand. From 1888 until the 1920s, Jack guided ships through Cook's Strait. People came from around the world to see him.

In 1978, a small fishing boat was lost off the coast of South Africa. It was caught in a thick fog and dangerous water. The fishermen told of four dolphins who led their boat to shore. Another newspaper account told of a ship that exploded. A woman was injured and thrown overboard. She said three dolphins swam near her and helped her float. They stayed with her until she could climb on a buoy. There are many other stories of dolphins saving drowning people by pushing them to shallow water.

1. Put these events in the order that they happened. What happened first? Write the number **1** on the line by that sentence. Then write the number **2** by the sentence that tells what happened next. Write the number **3** by the sentence that tells what happened last.

_____ The baby nurses for about 18 months.

_____ The mother pushes the baby to the surface.

_____ The other dolphins surround the mother.

_____ **2.** When did Plutarch praise dolphins?
  A. 300 years ago
  B. in 1888
  C. 2,000 years ago

_____ **3.** When do other dolphins surround a mother dolphin?
  A. while the mother dolphin gives birth
  B. while the mother nurses her baby
  C. while the mother pushes her baby to the surface

_____ **4.** When did Pelorus Jack guide ships through Cook's Strait?
  A. before Plutarch died
  B. before four dolphins helped some lost fishermen
  C. before dolphins were thought of as special animals

_____ **5.** When was a small fishing boat lost off the coast of South Africa?
  A. during the time when Pelorus Jack guided ships
  B. when a woman's ship exploded
  C. in 1978

Writing Roundup

Read the paragraph below. Think about the sequence, or time order. Answer the questions in complete sentences.

Andrew talked about how well he shot basketball free throws, so Chris challenged him to a contest. Andrew took his first shot, which bounced off the backboard. Next Andrew threw the ball to Chris. Chris took a shot, and the ball went in the basket. Then Andrew took a second shot, but it rolled off the rim. Chris's second shot went in. Andrew decided to get some tips from Chris.

1. When did Chris challenge Andrew to a free-throw contest?

_____

_____

2. What happened after Andrew took his first shot?

_____

_____

3. When did Chris take his first shot?

_____

_____

4. When did Andrew decide to get tips from Chris?

_____

_____

Prewriting

Think about something that you have done, such as doing your laundry, training to improve your fitness, or tie-dyeing a T-shirt. Write the events in sequence below.

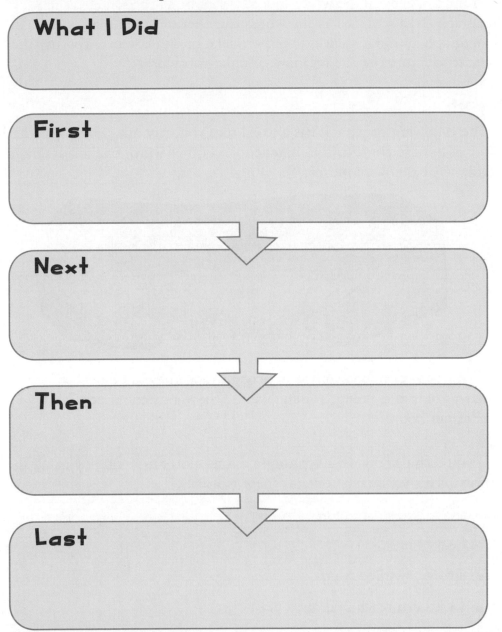

What I Did

First

Next

Then

Last

On Your Own

Now use another sheet of paper to write a paragraph about what you have done. Write the events in the order that they happened. Use time order words.

What Is Context?

Context means all the words in a sentence or all the sentences in a paragraph. In a sentence all the words together make up the context. In a paragraph all the sentences together make up the context. You use the context to figure out the meaning of unknown words.

Try It!

The following paragraph has a word that you may not know. See whether you can use the context (the sentences and other words in the paragraph) to decide what the word means.

Typhoons develop over warm ocean water. They are made of heavy rains and strong, swirling winds. The winds can reach 200 miles per hour.

If you don't know what **typhoons** means, you can decide by using the context. This paragraph contains these words:

Clue: develop over warm ocean water

Clue: heavy rains

Clue: strong, swirling winds

Clue: winds can reach 200 miles per hour

Find these clues in the paragraph and circle them. What words do you think of when you read the clues? You might think of *weather*. What other words do you think of? Write the words below:

_____

Did you write *storm* or *hurricane*? The context clue words tell you that a **typhoon** is a kind of storm like a hurricane.

Working with Context

This unit asks questions that you can answer by using context clues in paragraphs. There are two kinds of paragraphs. The paragraphs in the first part of this unit have blank spaces in them. You can use the context clues in the paragraphs to decide which words should go in each space. Here is an example:

Henry Ford built cars that everyone could buy. He cut down on the costs of ___1___. He passed the savings on to his ___2___.

___B___ 1. **A.** chatter   **B.** production   **C.** sleep   **D.** winter

_____ 2. **A.** towns   **B.** models   **C.** customers   **D.** cowards

Look at the answer choices for question 1. Try putting each choice in the paragraph to see which one makes the most sense. Treat the paragraph as a puzzle. Which pieces don't fit? It doesn't make sense for a car builder to cut down on the costs of *chatter*, *sleep*, or *winter*. You have decided what doesn't fit. The correct answer is *production*, answer **B**. Now try to answer question 2 on your own.

The paragraphs in the second part of this unit are different. For these you figure out the meaning of a word that is printed in **dark letters** in the paragraph. Here is an example:

The scientists studied the volcano carefully. There was a lump on its side. The lump was getting bigger. They knew that the volcano would **erupt** soon. They warned all the people who lived nearby to move before it blew up.

In this paragraph the word in dark type is **erupt**. Find the context clues, and treat the paragraph as a puzzle. Then choose a word that means the same as **erupt**.

_____ 3. In this paragraph, the word **erupt** means
        A. disappear   **C.** blow up
        B. get bigger   **D.** bring rain

Read the passages and answer the questions about context. Remember, context is a way to learn new words by thinking about the other words used in a story.

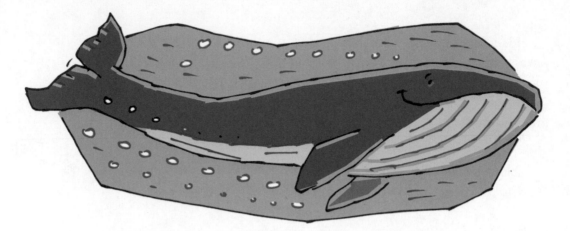

The great blue whale is bigger than the dinosaurs were. A human being could stand up straight inside a whale's ___1___ mouth. However, a whale's throat is very tiny. A whale could not ___2___ a person.

_____ 1. **A.** little   **B.** tremendous   **C.** hungry   **D.** tight

_____ 2. **A.** taste   **B.** capture   **C.** swallow   **D.** find

The game of tennis began around 800 hundred years ago. Players in France hit a ball over a net. However, they did not use a ___3___ to play the game. They used the ___4___ of their hands.

_____ 3. **A.** mask   **B.** motor   **C.** trap   **D.** racket

_____ 4. **A.** palms   **B.** nets   **C.** riddles   **D.** families

Your fingerprints are unlike those of any other person. Even twins have fingerprints that ___5___. Experts say that fingerprints are the best way to ___6___ someone. These prints can help solve crimes.

_____ 5. **A.** whisk   **B.** vary   **C.** flicker   **D.** advance

_____ 6. **A.** huddle   **B.** invite   **C.** grasp   **D.** identify

Scientists say that black holes ___7___ in space although they cannot be seen. It is thought that black holes ___8___ when huge stars cave in. If the Sun became a black hole, it would be only 4 miles across.

_____ 7. **A.** budge   **B.** gust   **C.** exist   **D.** lend

_____ 8. **A.** leak   **B.** satisfy   **C.** admire   **D.** develop

Florida is on the southeastern coast of the United States. It has water on three sides. Since the ___9___ is warm, there are many palm trees. There are also many beautiful beaches. For these reasons, many people take ___10___ in Florida.

_____ 9. **A.** climate   **B.** size   **C.** rowboat   **D.** insect

_____10. **A.** water   **B.** tests   **C.** vacations   **D.** lists

---

The first motion pictures were made in 1887. To see these movies, people looked through a hole in a box. Movies were later shown on a ___11___. Recordings were used for sound. Later, sound was put ___12___ on the movie film.

_____11. **A.** screen   **B.** oven   **C.** hive   **D.** tub

_____12. **A.** sadly   **B.** happily   **C.** directly   **D.** angrily

Artists often use colors to ___13___ feelings. Bright colors show happy feelings. Dark colors show sad feelings. When you look at a painting, you can tell what the artist's ___14___ was.

_____13. **A.** buy   **B.** eat   **C.** shovel   **D.** express

_____14. **A.** height   **B.** mood   **C.** brush   **D.** meal

---

Nothing lives or grows on the Moon, but scientists have discovered that some plants on Earth grow better if they are ___15___ by the Moon. If moon dust is ___16___ over the plants, they grow much bigger. No one yet knows why.

_____15. **A.** melted   **B.** aided   **C.** wet   **D.** arranged

_____16. **A.** trusted   **B.** curved   **C.** sprinkled   **D.** chosen

Red Jacket was a famous Native American in the 1700s. He helped the British soldiers. He ___**1**___ the Americans fighting against the British. A British ___**2**___ gave him a red jacket. That is how he got his name.

_____ 1. **A.** loved   **B.** rewarded   **C.** forgot   **D.** opposed

_____ 2. **A.** tea   **B.** officer   **C.** rifle   **D.** coat

---

Several things help broken bones get well fast. Young people seem to ___**3**___ faster than old people do, so the age of the ___**4**___ counts. It also helps to get the hurt person to a doctor as soon as possible.

_____ 3. **A.** yawn   **B.** level
           C. heal   **D.** bend

_____ 4. **A.** chapter   **B.** sheet
           C. doctor   **D.** patient

When roads were built, people threw dirt from each side of the road to the ___**5**___. This raised road came to be ___**6**___ a highway.

_____ 5. **A.** center   **B.** witch   **C.** apron   **D.** contest

_____ 6. **A.** parked   **B.** swept   **C.** showered   **D.** termed

---

Experts say that swimming is the best exercise. Swimming ___**7**___ your strength. Pushing your way through the water builds your muscles. This exercise is less ___**8**___ than most other sports. Swimmers are not hurt as often as are joggers and runners.

_____ 7. **A.** fails   **B.** tickles   **C.** improves   **D.** poisons

_____ 8. **A.** dangerous   **B.** correct   **C.** lazy   **D.** awake

The Statue of Liberty was ___9___ in many separate pieces. The pieces were packed in ___10___. Then they were shipped from France to America. There the pieces were joined to form Miss Liberty.

_____ 9. **A.** whole   **B.** originally   **C.** never   **D.** bent

_____10. **A.** beds   **B.** nickels   **C.** lights   **D.** crates

---

The first kites were made about 2,500 years ago in China. They were made of large leaves. String had not been ___11___ yet. The kite strings were made of twisted ___12___.

_____11. **A.** shown   **B.** liked   **C.** wanted   **D.** invented

_____12. **A.** vines   **B.** trees   **C.** tops   **D.** rows

---

Columbus found many ___13___ things to eat in the New World. When he went back to Europe, he carried some of these new foods with him. He gave the king and queen of Spain a ___14___. He offered them corn, peppers, pineapples, pumpkins, and sweet potatoes.

_____13. **A.** hidden   **B.** secret   **C.** short   **D.** delicious

_____14. **A.** banquet   **B.** carpet   **C.** princess   **D.** batter

---

Some people are ___15___ that mice scare elephants. However, these big beasts do not ___16___ fear when they see a mouse. Elephants will run away from a rabbit or a dog, though!

_____15. **A.** clear   **B.** comfortable   **C.** hopeful   **D.** convinced

_____16. **A.** enjoy   **B.** choose   **C.** exhibit   **D.** challenge

The first Olympic Games were held in Greece. Boys between the ages of 12 and 17 entered the junior ___1___. At the age of 18, they could enter the ___2___ contests.

_____ 1. **A.** schools   **B.** darkness   **C.** events   **D.** grounds

_____ 2. **A.** small   **B.** championship   **C.** fast   **D.** strange

Some bats have only one baby at a time. When the mother bat flies out at night, she carries her ___3___ along with her. The young one hangs onto the mother as she ___4___ through the dark.

_____ 3. **A.** amount   **B.** sister   **C.** newborn   **D.** enemy

_____ 4. **A.** swoops   **B.** blinks   **C.** motions   **D.** hatches

Plants need light in order to grow, but many plants ___5___ to grow fast in the dark. Corn is one ___6___. It grows most quickly during warm summer nights.

_____ 5. **A.** continue   **B.** burn   **C.** complete   **D.** dip

_____ 6. **A.** flower   **B.** field   **C.** example   **D.** weed

On the ___7___ person's head, there are about 100,000 hairs. When people are young, their hair grows fast. It grows about one-hundredth of an inch per day. This ___8___ growth slows down as people get older. If you never cut your hair in your life, it might grow to be 25 feet long.

_____ 7. **A.** neat   **B.** old   **C.** average   **D.** noisy

_____ 8. **A.** hard   **B.** rapid   **C.** sleepy   **D.** straight

Young Mozart never went to school. His father ___**9**___ him in music and math at home. By the time he was five, Mozart was writing his own music for the piano. A year later he played his ___**10**___ for people all over Europe.

_____ **9.** **A.** tried   **B.** found   **C.** paid   **D.** tutored

_____ **10.** **A.** compositions   **B.** lanes   **C.** lessons   **D.** ideas

There are 50 states in the United States. Alaska and Hawaii ___**11**___ no states at all. Maine touches only one other state. Both Missouri and Tennessee are ___**12**___ by eight other states.

_____ **11.** **A.** defend   **B.** border   **C.** cross   **D.** show

_____ **12.** **A.** covered   **B.** owned   **C.** held   **D.** surrounded

On April Fool's Day, some people make ___**13**___ calls to zoos, so many zoos unplug their telephones. The zoo workers are busy. They can't ___**14**___ time taking messages for Mr. Fish, Mrs. Bear, and Miss Lion!

_____ **13.** **A.** helpful   **B.** ridiculous   **C.** beautiful   **D.** new

_____ **14.** **A.** hurry   **B.** tell   **C.** waste   **D.** count

You have probably heard about people who ___**15**___ stamps, signs, strings, buttons, or fire hats. You never know what ___**16**___ and silly things people want to save.

_____ **15.** **A.** collect   **B.** carve   **C.** manage   **D.** return

_____ **16.** **A.** tough   **B.** comfortable   **C.** unusual   **D.** lively

Dragons still live. The Komodo dragon in Asia is the largest living ___1___. It grows to be more than 10 feet long. It has a long tail, ___2___ skin, and a wide red mouth.

_____ 1. **A.** western   **B.** visitor   **C.** puppet   **D.** lizard

_____ 2. **A.** thirsty   **B.** sweet   **C.** rough   **D.** private

Exercise can help people live longer. ___3___ say that people who walk or run about half an hour each day stay in better ___4___. Some people say they don't have time to work out. They should take the time. For each hour a person exercises, that person may live an hour longer.

_____ 3. **A.** Owners   **B.** Elephants   **C.** Experts   **D.** Uncles

_____ 4. **A.** sunshine   **B.** order   **C.** matter   **D.** health

A woman said to a friend, "Yesterday I fell over 40 feet." The friend ___5___, "That's just ___6___! Were you hurt?" The first woman said, "No, I was just finding my seat at the movies."

_____ 5. **A.** felt   **B.** exclaimed   **C.** discovered   **D.** bounced

_____ 6. **A.** horrible   **B.** favor   **C.** silent   **D.** aboard

Some gardeners like to ___7___ huge plants. Farmers in Alaska enter contests. They see whose cabbages are largest. A man in New England raised giant ___8___. They weighed 580 pounds each!

_____ 7. **A.** cultivate   **B.** send
         C. ride   **D.** mail

_____ 8. **A.** fields   **B.** feasts
         C. pumpkins   **D.** ants

The unicorn is an imaginary beast. It is supposed to have a __9__ horn that twists out of the middle of its forehead. In pictures it is __10__ as having the head and body of a horse, the beard of a goat, the legs of a deer, and the tail of a lion.

_____ **9. A.** spiral　　**B.** buffalo　　**C.** button　　**D.** flat

_____ **10. A.** born　　**B.** portrayed　　**C.** divided　　**D.** touched

A mountain is worn down year by year. Some of the rocks on the mountain have cracks in them. Water goes into the cracks. As the water freezes, it __11__ . This causes the cracks to get larger. Then the rocks are __12__ by wind and more water.

_____ **11. A.** expands　　**B.** replies　　**C.** goes　　**D.** aims

_____ **12. A.** dared　　**B.** gone　　**C.** seen　　**D.** weathered

Deborah Sampson dressed up as a man. She did this so she could join an army __13__ during the American Revolution. In one battle she was wounded in the __14__ . She removed the bullet herself. That way no one discovered that she was a woman.

_____ **13. A.** ax　　**B.** regiment　　**C.** knife　　**D.** park

_____ **14. A.** mitten　　**B.** suitcase　　**C.** rope　　**D.** thigh

Seamounts are __15__ cones, or mountains, that rise up from the bottom of the sea. They can be thousands of feet high and still be far below the surface of the water. They are entirely __16__ in the ocean.

_____ **15. A.** spicy　　**B.** awful　　**C.** volcanic　　**D.** easy

_____ **16. A.** killed　　**B.** proved　　**C.** loose　　**D.** submerged

The honeysucker, or honey possum, eats the **nectar** found in large flowers. To do this it sticks its long, thin nose into a flower. Then it uses its long, rough tongue to get the sticky food.

_____ **1.** In this paragraph, the word **nectar** means
  A. fruit   **C.** sweet liquid
  B. roots   **D.** green leaves

Long ago, a feast was more than just fancy food on a table. People dressed in fine clothing. Guests were often **entertained** with music, dancing, and juggling.

_____ **2.** In this paragraph, the word **entertained** means
  A. starved   **C.** invited
  B. seated   **D.** amused

People have always feared the blasts of hot lava and ashes from a volcano. The power of a volcano has caused many disasters. In 1991, the explosion of a volcano in the Philippine Islands **demolished** an air force base. The base was completely covered with hot ash.

_____ **3.** In this paragraph, the word **demolished** means
  A. built   **C.** destroyed
  B. visited   **D.** landed

A boomerang is made so that it returns to the person who throws it. A boomerang has two arms and a **curve** in the middle. This shape makes the boomerang spin. This spinning causes the boomerang to circle back to the person who threw it.

_____ **4.** In this paragraph, the word **curve** means
  A. leg   **C.** belt
  B. well   **D.** bend

Some people fear alligators, but there are not many **authentic** cases of alligators attacking people. Most reports have not been backed by facts.

_____ **5.** In this paragraph, the word **authentic** means

    A. long   **C.** real

    B. thin   **D.** lengthy

You will find few birds in the deepest, darkest part of a forest. Birds like a **habitat** near the edge of the forest. There is more food for them there.

_____ **6.** In this paragraph, the word **habitat** means

    A. sunshine   **C.** cage

    B. home   **D.** insect

You know that the "home on the range" is "where the deer and the antelope play." However, no animal in North America fits the true **classification** of antelope.

_____ **7.** In this paragraph, the word **classification** means

    A. friendliness   **C.** particular group

    B. kind of music   **D.** surrounding land

Some people who are good at **archery** like to enter contests. They aim their arrows at a target. It is divided into colored rings. An arrow that hits the center circle is worth 10 points.

_____ **8.** In this paragraph, the word **archery** means

    A. running   **C.** public speaking

    B. swimming   **D.** arrow shooting

When ducks **migrate** south each fall, many of them pass over Stuttgard, Arkansas, so the people there hold a duck-calling contest. As the ducks fly by, the people quack away!

_____ **1.** In this paragraph, the word **migrate** means
    A. locate   **C.** travel
    B. mumble   **D.** honk

Have you ever seen a moonbow? It's like a rainbow, but it's made by the moon. Moonbows **occur** when the moon's light shines through the mist from a waterfall.

_____ **2.** In this paragraph, the word **occur** means
    A. rain   **C.** happen
    B. flow   **D.** disappear

In the middle of Enterprise, Alabama, stands a **monument**. It is shaped like an insect called the boll weevil. This insect once ate all the cotton plants in Enterprise, so people decided to grow peanuts. They earned more money with peanuts. That's why they honored the boll weevil.

_____ **3.** In this paragraph, the word **monument** means
    A. statue   **C.** tree
    B. farm   **D.** plant

Every June **mobs** of people gather at Jensen Beach in Florida to watch for sea turtles. Hundreds of people snap pictures of the turtles as they lay their eggs.

_____ **4.** In this paragraph, the word **mobs** means
    A. crowds   **C.** swimmers
    B. visitors   **D.** couples

Clowns spend much time painting their faces. They don't want people to copy their design. Pictures of the clowns' faces are put in a file as a **permanent** record.

_____ **5.** In this paragraph, the word **permanent** means
     A. playing   **C.** lasting
     B. pretty   **D.** broken

A **typical** American saying is *O.K.* There are many stories about how this saying got started. One story is that some writers in Boston were having fun. They used *O.K.* to stand for "oll korrect," a misspelling of "all correct."

_____ **6.** In this paragraph, the word **typical** means
     A. common   **C.** wild
     B. west   **D.** odd

Shirley Temple won an Oscar award for her **performance** in the movie *Bright Eyes*. She was in this movie when she was only six years old.

_____ **7.** In this paragraph, the word **performance** means
     A. youth   **C.** acting
     B. sewing   **D.** dinner

The town of Young America, Minnesota, **sponsors** a bed-racing contest each year. People line up all sorts of beds on wheels. Then they roll them down the main street toward the finish line.

_____ **8.** In this paragraph, the word **sponsors** means
     A. owns   **C.** sells
     B. wins   **D.** holds

Libraries have **revealed** some interesting facts about books that are returned. One librarian reported that socks were often left in books. Another librarian found a peanut butter sandwich in a returned book!

_____ **1.** In this paragraph, the word **revealed** means
    A. made known   **C.** torn down
    B. kept hidden   **D.** laughed at

A lizard has a forked tongue. The tongue has two **functions**. The lizard both touches and smells with it.

_____ **2.** In this paragraph, the word **functions** means
    A. tests   **C.** teeth
    B. purposes   **D.** leads

Some animals can **resemble** other things. This helps keep them safe from enemies. For instance, the treehopper looks just like a thorn on a rosebush. Birds may like to eat treehoppers, but it's hard for birds to find them.

_____ **3.** In this paragraph, the word **resemble** means
    A. see like   **C.** look like
    B. report to   **D.** differ from

Rain forests grow where it is warm and wet all year. Thick trees and vines form a high **canopy** over the forest. As a result, little sunlight reaches the forest floor.

_____ **4.** In this paragraph, the word **canopy** means
    A. cloud   **C.** capitol
    B. covering   **D.** night

Many people wear black as a sign of **mourning**. In China the color for death is white. People in Turkey wear purple. Everywhere, people follow special customs when someone dies.

_____ **5.** In this paragraph, the word **mourning** means
- **A.** seeing dawn
- **C.** showing joy
- **B.** feeling sick
- **D.** showing sadness

The most common **source** of milk is the cow. The goat also gives milk. Other animals that give milk are the camel, buffalo, yak, reindeer, llama, and zebra.

_____ **6.** In this paragraph, the word **source** means
- **A.** bottle
- **B.** direction
- **C.** drink
- **D.** supply

When Franz Liszt played the piano, he became **violent**. Often the keys would fly off the piano. Sometimes the strings of the piano would snap with the force of his blows.

_____ **7.** In this paragraph, the word **violent** means
- **A.** rough
- **C.** gentle
- **B.** purple
- **D.** large

In 1608, Thomas Coryat brought a new custom to England. He had learned how to eat with a fork. At first the English didn't think this new way to eat was **appropriate**. They did not think it was a good idea. They did not begin to use forks until some time later.

_____ **8.** In this paragraph, the word **appropriate** means
- **A.** fun
- **C.** filling
- **B.** correct
- **D.** magic

Most animals that live in the sea have layers of fat to keep them warm. Sea otters have thick, furry coats instead. Their coats are so **effective** against the cold that they stay warm even in cold water.

_____ 1. In this paragraph, the word **effective** means
  A. chilly
  B. successful
  C. hot
  D. wet

Before airplanes, trains were common. They moved people and freight long distances. As years went by, air and highway travel became easier. Then train use **declined**.

_____ 2. In this paragraph, the word **declined** means
  A. grew   C. rose
  B. dropped   D. rushed

Henry Ford didn't invent the factory, but he improved it. Ford used **conveyors** that brought parts to the workers as they stood in their places.

_____ 3. In this paragraph, the word **conveyors** means
  A. mattresses   C. types of small airplanes
  B. skilled workers   D. means of carrying things

The oldest false teeth are almost 3,000 years old. They were found on the body of a **deceased** person in an old grave. The teeth were strung together with gold wire.

_____ 4. In this paragraph, the word **deceased** means
  A. dead   C. healthy
  B. old   D. rich

Long ago a bride's father gave all her shoes to her new husband. This **indicated** that the father no longer had to care for the bride. Today we recall this custom by tying shoes to a wedding car.

_____ **5.** In this paragraph, the word **indicated** means

    A. behaved   **C.** prayed

    B. pained   **D.** meant

In spite of its name, banana oil isn't **derived** from bananas. It is made from chemicals that are mixed in a laboratory. The smell of the oil is like the smell of a banana.

_____ **6.** In this paragraph, the word **derived** means

    A. taken   **C.** grown

    B. slippery   **D.** pasted

The bits of paper thrown during parades are called confetti. This word means "candy." Once people threw candy during **festive** and merry events. Now we throw paper.

_____ **7.** In this paragraph, the word **festive** means

    A. worn   **C.** smooth

    B. tasty   **D.** jolly

Astronauts have a big problem when traveling in space. In space, water does not pour. Drops of water just float around. Astronauts must use special **methods** for getting clean. They can't take regular baths or showers. They must wash with special equipment.

_____ **8.** In this paragraph, the word **methods** means

    A. brushes   **C.** ways

    B. ideas   **D.** tubs

Writing Roundup

Read each paragraph. Write a word that makes sense on each line.

Darrell was reading a book about an adventure

on a ranch. "I hope this book has an ending that's

(1) _____," he said. "Some adventure

books are **(2)** _____."

Tamika had practiced for weeks, but still she felt

(3) _____ because she had never

played her violin in public. She hoped the audience

would like her **(4)** _____.

What an ice storm we had last winter! The **(5)** _____

was off for several hours. We had to use **(6)** _____ to

light our way around the house.

Read each paragraph. Write a sentence that makes sense on each line.

Ms. Dixon's class was making shoebox models of
a scene at the bottom of the ocean. Akiko wanted to include
seashells, but they didn't have any. What could they use?

(1) _____.

They needed fish, and Leslie had an idea for that.

(2) _____.

Ryan suggested a way to make the scene look more real.

(3) _____.

The parade was coming! Daniel jumped up and down with
excitement. What would he see first as the parade rounded
the corner? (4) _____

_____. At last, there it was!

(5) _____.

That was fun to see, but Daniel's favorite part of the parade
turned out to be something else. (6) _____

_____.

What Is a Main Idea?

The main idea of a paragraph tells what the paragraph is about. All the other sentences are details that add to the main idea. The main idea sentence is often the first or last sentence in the paragraph. You may find the main idea sentence in the middle of the paragraph too.

This example may help you think about main ideas:

$$3 \quad + \quad 4 \quad + \quad 5 \quad = \quad 12$$

detail + detail + detail = main idea

The *3*, *4*, and *5* are like details. They are smaller than their sum, *12*. The *12*, like the main idea, is bigger. It is made up of several smaller parts.

Try It!

Read this story and underline the main idea sentence.

Small dogs usually live longer than big dogs. The tiny Pekingese can live to be 20 years old. The giant Saint Bernard rarely lives as long as 14 years.

The main idea sentence is the first sentence in the story. The other sentences are details about the main idea sentence.

The main idea could come at the end of the paragraph:

The tiny Pekingese can live to be 20 years old. The giant Saint Bernard rarely lives as long as 14 years. Small dogs usually live longer than big dogs.

Practice Finding the Main Idea

This unit asks you to find main ideas of paragraphs. Read the paragraph and answer the question below.

The monarch butterfly makes a long trip south each fall. Some butterflies fly almost 1,800 miles from the northern United States to Mexico. As spring warms the air, the butterflies begin to return. The butterflies lay their eggs and then die. The young return to the north to start the cycle over again.

___D___ **1.** The story mainly tells
   A. which butterflies make the trip
   B. how far the insects fly
   C. when butterflies lay their eggs
   D. what the monarch's long trip is like

The correct answer is **D.** The first sentence says, "The monarch butterfly makes a long trip south each fall." This is the main idea sentence. The other sentences give details about the trip.

Sometimes a paragraph does not have a main idea sentence. Then it is made up only of details. Read the story below and answer the question. Write the letter of your answer in the blank.

The front part of a newspaper contains important stories of national and local events. The sports pages report scores and give information about players, coaches, and teams. The comics section makes many people laugh.

_____ **2.** The story mainly tells
   A. what the front section contains
   B. where you can read about players
   C. about different parts of a newspaper
   D. what makes people laugh

Read each passage. After each passage you will answer a question about the main idea of the passage. Remember, the main idea is the main point in a story.

1. Scientists are teaching gorillas how to talk. The apes' names are Koko and Michael. Although their mouths and throats are not made for speaking, they can talk with their hands. They use Ameslan, which is a sign language some deaf people use. Koko and Michael can say more than 500 words and can understand at least 1,000.

_____ 1. The story mainly tells
  A. how to use Ameslan
  B. how Koko and Michael talk
  C. how scientists are studying gorillas
  D. how apes are like human children

2. Today there are gyms for people who use wheelchairs. These people can lift weights or do other exercises. Teams of people can get together for a game of basketball. Being in a wheelchair doesn't have to mean just sitting around!

_____ 2. The story mainly tells
  A. how some people use wheelchairs
  B. where people in wheelchairs can exercise
  C. how to work out for good health
  D. how to lift weights on special machines

3. Sim One is an unusual robot. *Sim* is short for *simulator*, which means "a thing that imitates something real." In this case, Sim One imitates a living human being. It looks like a man. It has teeth, hair, and even blinking eyelids. It has a heart that beats and a chest that moves up and down when it breathes. Everything is controlled by a computer. Doctors use Sim One to teach students how to care for people who are ill.

_____ **3.** The story mainly tells
- **A.** about the many different kinds of robots
- **B.** how doctors teach students
- **C.** what Sim One is like
- **D.** how computers control breathing

4. Cats are very hard to train, but some people have figured out how to do it. The secret is that a cat's brain is in its stomach. All you need is cat food, a spoon, and plenty of time! Put some food on the spoon and hold it wherever you want the cat to go. The cat will learn to obey your hand motions, even when there isn't any food.

_____ **4.** The story mainly tells
- **A.** how to teach an old dog new tricks
- **B.** where the parts of a cat are located
- **C.** how to train a cat
- **D.** the differences between cats and dogs

5. The sport of logrolling was invented by lumberjacks. Lumberjacks are workers who cut down trees and float the logs down the river to the lumber mills. For fun, these people hold contests. Two lumberjacks stand on a log in the river and try to make each other fall off by rolling the log with their feet.

_____ **5.** The story mainly tells
- **A.** about the sport of logrolling
- **B.** where lumberjacks work
- **C.** how to float logs
- **D.** where to saw lumber

1. Comic books appeared in 1920. The first ones were only collections of comic strips that had been in the newspaper. Later someone wrote new stories instead of using the old strips. The first all-new comic book was a detective story. It was very popular. In June 1938, the first *Superman* comic book was printed. Comic books quickly became part of the American way of life.

_____ **1.** The story mainly tells
  A. when *Superman* comic books were first printed
  B. how comic strips looked in newspapers
  C. how comic books developed
  D. when a detective story became popular

---

2. Certain facts help people know what the weather will be. For instance, weather patterns move from west to east. This happens because Earth turns to the east, and the wind often blows from the west. Also, Earth tilts on its axis. The part that leans toward the Sun is always warmer than the part that leans away.

_____ **2.** The story mainly tells
  A. how people determine weather patterns
  B. why the Sun is warmer
  C. why the wind blows
  D. why Earth tilts

---

3. "Learning the ropes" comes from the sport of sailing. Some sailboats have so many ropes that they look like spiderwebs. Some of the ropes keep the mast from leaning too much into the wind. Sailors use other ropes to adjust the sails. Sailing is easy, once you learn the ropes!

_____ **3.** The story mainly tells
  A. how to sail
  B. about the ropes on a sailboat
  C. how boats change directions
  D. how the mast works

4. Richard Byrd was a famous explorer. He was the first person to fly over both the North and South Poles. He once spent five months alone in a hut studying Antarctica. The temperature was 70 degrees below zero, and he almost froze to death. However, he lived and continued exploring for many more years.

_____ **4.** The story mainly tells
- **A.** how to explore Antarctica
- **B.** why Richard Byrd is remembered
- **C.** when to fly over the North Pole
- **D.** how to keep from freezing to death

5. Kids have been racing in the Soap Box Derby since 1934. The kids must build their own cars, but they can get help from their parents. The kids get companies to pay for the things they need. In return, the kids paint the company's name on their car. The cars don't have engines. Instead, they roll down a hill.

_____ **5.** The story mainly tells
- **A.** about kids and the Soap Box Derby
- **B.** how the power of gravity moves cars
- **C.** how long the Soap Box Derby is
- **D.** how parents help in the Soap Box Derby

1. Whitcomb Judson won a patent for a device. He called it the "clasp-locker." He showed it at the 1893 World's Fair, but it didn't attract any interest. Twenty years later Gideon Sundback improved the device. He renamed it the "hook-less fastener." Then B. F. Goodrich put the fastener on boots. He named it for the sound it made. Z-i-p! Now everyone calls the device a "zipper." It sounds a lot better than "clasp-locker."

_____ **1.** The story mainly tells

    A. that Judson won a patent

    B. when the World's Fair took place

    C. who Gideon Sundback was

    D. how a device got its name from the sound it made

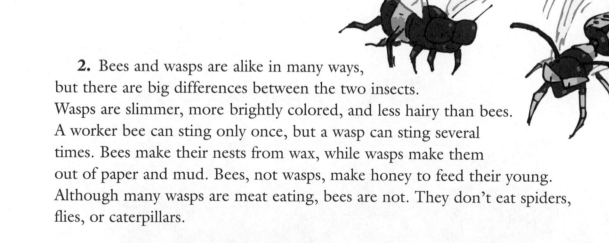

2. Bees and wasps are alike in many ways, but there are big differences between the two insects. Wasps are slimmer, more brightly colored, and less hairy than bees. A worker bee can sting only once, but a wasp can sting several times. Bees make their nests from wax, while wasps make them out of paper and mud. Bees, not wasps, make honey to feed their young. Although many wasps are meat eating, bees are not. They don't eat spiders, flies, or caterpillars.

_____ **2.** The story mainly tells

    A. about the ways that bees and wasps are alike

    B. how bees and wasps are different

    C. how bees build their nests

    D. why wasps and bees sting

3. A human baby is born without teeth. As an adult he or she will have 32 permanent teeth. A baby grows a set of 20 baby teeth before a set of permanent teeth. One by one, the baby teeth fall out as the permanent teeth begin to appear. By the age of 25, a person has a full set of 32 permanent teeth.

_____ **3.** The story mainly tells
- **A.** about baby and permanent teeth
- **B.** what teeth are made of
- **C.** at what age baby teeth are lost
- **D.** how long it takes teeth to grow

---

4. The year 1972 was important for Yvonne Burke. It was the year in which she turned 40, got married, and ran for the United States Congress. She was selected Woman of the Year by the *Los Angeles Times* and the National Association of Black Manufacturers. She was also named as one of America's 200 future leaders by *Time* magazine.

_____ **4.** The story mainly tells that
- **A.** 1972 was a difficult year for Burke
- **B.** Burke won election to the Senate
- **C.** 1972 was a successful year for Burke
- **D.** Burke was *Time* magazine's Woman of the Year

---

5. Sand is made up of millions of tiny, loose, and gritty pieces of rock. The rocks are broken down by wind, rain, frost, or water. The rubbing away of the rocks wears them down into the tiny grains found on the beach. Sand is coarser than dust but finer than gravel. It's made up mostly of quartz, mica, and feldspar.

_____ **5.** The story mainly tells
- **A.** the many uses of sand
- **B.** how rocks are worn down into sand
- **C.** how many rocks it takes to make sand
- **D.** about the size of a grain of sand

1. Did you know that when a sheep falls down, it cannot get up again by itself? A sheep has a heavy body but delicate legs. When it's lying on its back, it's weighted down by its thick, heavy fleece. Even waving its legs doesn't help. Its legs are too thin and weak to swing its heavy body onto its side. A shepherd has to help the sheep back onto its feet!

_____ **1.** The story mainly tells
   A. how a sheep uses its legs to get up
   B. that a sheep never falls down
   C. why a sheep can't get itself up when it falls down
   D. how a sheep uses its fleece to get up

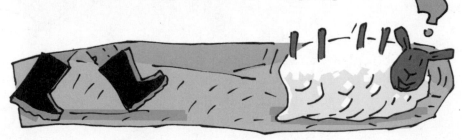

2. Are you one of those people who is bothered by mosquitoes? If you are, there are ways to help prevent mosquitoes from biting. Dark colors and rough textures attract mosquitoes. If you will be outdoors, wear pale, smooth clothing instead of jeans. Some scents attract mosquitoes, so don't wear perfume or aftershave lotion. Be careful about the shampoo you use. Even scented shampoo can attract a bite!

_____ **2.** The story mainly tells
   A. why mosquitoes bite
   B. why mosquito bites itch
   C. how to prevent mosquitoes from biting
   D. how mosquitoes are attracted to yellow clothing

3. There is an easy way to find out how far away a thunderstorm is from you. Count the number of seconds between the flash of lightning and the clap of thunder. Then divide this number by five. This will tell you about how many miles away the lightning has struck. If you see the flash and hear the thunder at the same time, the storm is directly overhead.

_____ **3.** The story mainly tells
   A. how to find out how far away a thunderstorm is
   B. where lightning and thunder come from
   C. how to guess when a thunderstorm will end
   D. how to figure out the direction of a storm

4. How can bloodhounds pick up and follow the scents of missing people? Bloodhounds have a very keen sense of smell. A person's body sheds about 50 million skin cells a day. It releases about 30 to 50 ounces of moisture in the form of sweat. When bacteria mix with skin cells and sweat, a scent is produced. As a person moves, the scent is left on things such as grass and bushes. Bloodhounds can smell this. They have rescued many people.

_____ **4.** The story mainly tells

    A. how bloodhounds can follow a person's scent

    B. how people sweat every day

    C. that bloodhounds have their own scent

    D. that bloodhounds don't have a sense of smell

---

5. The Cullinan Diamond is the largest diamond ever found. It weighed more than 1 ¼ pounds. It was found in a mine in South Africa. It was sent to King Edward II of England. The Cullinan Diamond was cut into 105 separate diamonds. Among these was the largest stone, the 530-carat Star of Africa. Today it is one of the British crown jewels.

_____ **5.** The story mainly tells

    A. how King Edward II found a large diamond

    B. about the largest diamond ever found

    C. that the diamond is a British crown jewel

    D. that there aren't any diamonds in South Africa

1. In 1823, a man in Ohio checked out a library book, but he forgot to return it. In 1968, the man's great-grandson returned the book to the library. It was 145 years late! Of course, the library did not make the great-grandson pay the fine. The overdue fine would have been $2,264!

_____ **1.** The story mainly tells
  A. about a man who decided to keep a library book
  B. about a library book that was 145 years past due
  C. about a man who paid a library fine
  D. when to return overdue library books

2. Daniel Defoe wrote a book called *The Adventures of Robinson Crusoe.* It was about a man who lived on a deserted island. Did you know that there was a real-life Robinson Crusoe, only his name was Alexander Selkirk? Selkirk was a sailor on a ship. One day he had a fight with its captain. He left the ship and stayed on an island off the coast of Chile. Selkirk lived on the deserted island for more than four years. Defoe heard about Selkirk's experience. He used Selkirk's adventures as a model to write his story about Robinson Crusoe.

_____ **2.** The story mainly tells that
  A. Crusoe was a real person
  B. Daniel Defoe met Alexander Selkirk
  C. the story of Crusoe was based on Selkirk's life
  D. Defoe lived on a deserted island

3. Harry S Truman was the president of the United States. When Truman was born, his parents couldn't agree on a middle name. Both of his grandfathers' names began with the letter *S*. Truman's parents couldn't decide on a name, so they used *S*. However, it doesn't have a period after it. The *S* in Harry S Truman is a middle name, not an initial.

_____ **3.** The story mainly tells that
    A. Harry Truman's middle name is S
    B. Harry S Truman was named after his father
    C. Harry S Truman didn't have a middle name
    D. Harry S Truman's parents agreed on everything

---

4. Doctors have found that smiling is good for your health. It puts you in a good mood. It could help keep your immune system strong. Luckily, smiling is very easy to do. It takes only 17 muscles to smile, while it takes 43 to frown.

_____ **4.** The story mainly tells
    A. how smiling is good for your health
    B. what makes a good mood
    C. about the immune system
    D. how muscles work

---

5. What is the most popular street name in the United States? Most people might think it's *Main Street*, but *Main* isn't even in the top three. The U.S. Postal Service claims that *Park* is the most common name. *Washington* is second in popularity. *Maple* is the third most common name in the country.

_____ **5.** The story mainly tells that
    A. *Main* is the least popular street name
    B. nobody knows what the most popular name is
    C. *Maple* is the most popular street name
    D. *Park* is the most popular street name

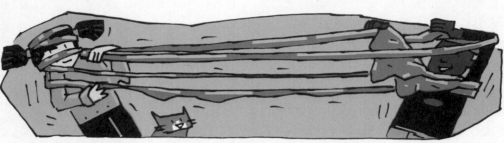

1. James Wright was trying to invent something to replace rubber. He put some acid into a test tube of oil. It produced something that bounced better than a rubber ball. It was stretchable and great fun. It was called Silly Putty and sold better than anything except crayons.

_____ 1. The story mainly tells
A. how James Wright invented rubber
B. why Silly Putty is sold in an egg-shaped box
C. how the first Silly Putty didn't bounce
D. how Silly Putty was invented

2. When Millard Fillmore was 19, he could hardly read or write. He lived on a farm. He spent more time working than going to school. Later he decided to return to school. Abigail Powers was Fillmore's teacher. They fell in love, and later they were married. Fillmore went on to become a teacher, a lawyer, and the president of the United States!

_____ 2. The story mainly tells that
A. Fillmore never learned to read and write
B. Fillmore had a successful life
C. Fillmore taught Abigail Powers to read
D. Fillmore never married

3. In 1849, a mapmaker in Alaska was working on a map of the coastline. None of his maps showed a name for one of the capes. A cape is a point of land that juts out into the sea. So he wrote *Name?* on the map and sent it to his mapmaking company in England. A worker at the map company thought the man had written *Nome* on the map. Since then the city on that cape has been known as Nome, Alaska.

_____ 3. The story mainly tells
A. how maps are made
B. how Nome, Alaska, got its name
C. how the mapmaker traveled around Alaska
D. how Alaska got its name

4. When Katherine Dunham was in college, she went to Haiti. There she studied the country's native dances. When she returned to the United States, she formed a group of African American dancers. They traveled around the world, performing the native dances of different countries. Today Dunham is recognized as one of the pioneers of African American dance.

_____ **4.** The story mainly tells that
- **A.** Dunham was from Haiti
- **B.** Dunham was a pioneer in Haiti
- **C.** Dunham was a pioneer in African American dance
- **D.** Dunham studied the food of Haiti

5. What does a music conductor do at a concert? The conductor's hands and arms tell the musicians what to do. The right hand keeps the beat. At the same time, movements of the left hand might show the violins when to join in. Musicians watch to see when to play faster or more softly. Sometimes it looks as if the conductor's arms are about to take flight, but that is the special way the conductor creates a musical story.

_____ **5.** The story mainly tells
- **A.** how a music conductor creates a musical story
- **B.** which of the conductor's hands keeps the beat
- **C.** why musicians watch the conductor
- **D.** when the violins join in

1. Hurricanes and tornadoes can whirl all kinds of creatures in the air and carry them for miles. At one time fish rained down on a town in Scotland. The storm had blown in from the Atlantic. Another time people in England felt bugs and frogs falling from the sky after a big storm.

_____ 1. The story mainly tells
  A. how fish fell from the sky
  B. what hurricanes and tornadoes can do
  C. what strange things fall from the sky
  D. how England had a big storm

2. Trevor Ferrell was just 13 years old, but he wanted to help homeless people. Trevor took food and clothes to the homeless living in his city. Other people heard what he was doing and wanted to help too. Now people are doing Trevor's work in many cities!

_____ 2. The story mainly tells
  A. about the problems of the world
  B. how Trevor Ferrell felt
  C. why people are without food, clothes, and shelter
  D. how Trevor Ferrell helped homeless people

3. The Great Salt Lake in Utah is bigger than the whole state of Delaware. Thousands of years ago, it was 10 times bigger than it is today. Over the years, the water has dried up. People at one time thought that the lake would disappear. Now the water is too high. Each spring it floods nearby towns.

_____ **3.** The story mainly tells
  A. why you should visit the state of Utah
  B. how the Great Salt Lake has changed in size
  C. why the Great Salt Lake is salty
  D. how big Delaware is

---

4. Mae Jemison became a doctor to help others. She joined the Peace Corps and brought medical aid to people in poor countries. Later this African American doctor joined the astronaut program. She took part in experiments on the space shuttle *Endeavor*. When Mae Jemison left the space program, she went back to helping people who are poor.

_____ **4.** The story mainly tells
  A. about Mae Jemison's life
  B. when Jemison joined the Peace Corps
  C. how Jemison became an astronaut
  D. which space shuttle Jemison went on

---

5. Some children are full of pep in the morning but get tired after lunch. Others don't even feel awake until two or three o'clock in the afternoon. Studies show that many children learn best during the middle of the afternoon, but that's the time when the school day is over! Perhaps someday children will be able to go to school when their "learning clock" says that the time is right.

_____ **5.** The story mainly tells
  A. how children feel during the day
  B. why children fall asleep in class
  C. why clocks tell time differently
  D. when schools will start in the future

1. Once Native Americans made beads from seashells. They called the beads "wampum." Wampum was used for many things. Wampum belts were special. Native Americans recorded agreements on them. First they cut the beads from shells. Next they drilled holes in the beads and rolled them smooth. Then they wove the beads into a belt that told the story of an agreement. For an important agreement, most of the beads were purple.

_____ **1.** The story mainly tells
  A. how beads were called wampum
  B. how purple beads were used
  C. how fabric was woven
  D. about a particular use for wampum

2. Isabella Baumfree was born a slave. When New York outlawed slavery, her master would not set her free, so Baumfree escaped. She changed her name to Sojourner Truth. She chose the name because she hoped to speak out against slavery. Truth traveled all over the North, spreading her message against slavery. Finally Truth lived to see the day in which slavery was outlawed throughout the country.

_____ **2.** The story mainly tells
  A. that Truth lived in New York
  B. that Truth fought to end slavery everywhere
  C. the year in which slavery was outlawed
  D. that Isabella Baumfree was a slave all her life

3. Movie stars were the first people to wear sunglasses. Early movie lights were very bright and hurt people's eyes. Actors wore sunglasses to rest their eyes. Today sunglasses are very popular. People wear them to protect their eyes from the sun.

_____ **3.** The story mainly tells
  A. how sunglasses were made
  B. who invented sunglasses
  C. why movie stars wore sunglasses
  D. that movie stars wanted to look mysterious

4. During World War I, the White House gardeners joined the army. To keep the White House lawn from looking uncared for, President Wilson bought a flock of sheep to eat the grass. Mrs. Wilson sold the sheep's wool. She made more than $100,000 and presented it as a gift to the Red Cross.

_____ **4.** The story mainly tells
- **A.** how a flock of sheep helped the Wilsons
- **B.** that Mrs. Wilson was a shepherd
- **C.** that gardeners did not have to serve in the army
- **D.** that President Wilson spent $100,000 on wool

5. During the 1850s, Levi Strauss moved to San Francisco. He sold canvas material used for making tents and covered wagons. Gold miners and railroad workers complained that their pants tore easily or became worn too soon. Strauss used his canvas to make a pair of pants. He called the pants after himself, or Levi's. They sold for 22¢ per pair. Later Strauss made a pair of denim pants and dyed them blue.

_____ **5.** The story mainly tells
- **A.** why Levi Strauss moved to San Francisco
- **B.** that Levi Strauss was a gold miner
- **C.** that the first Levi's were brown
- **D.** that Levi Strauss invented the first blue jeans

Writing Roundup

Read each paragraph. Think about the main idea. Write the main idea in your own words.

1. One bad taste is bad news for birds. In a test, birds were fed worms that would make them sick. After that the birds wouldn't eat the same type of worm even though there was nothing wrong with it. The birds lost an important food source.

What is the main idea of this paragraph?

_____

_____

2. If you see a live rattlesnake, stay away from it. If you see a dead rattlesnake, stay away from it too. Doctors in Arizona looked at the records of 34 people who had snake bites. Five people were bitten by dead snakes. Snakes can strike and bite for an hour or so after death. In fact, two people were bitten by the snake heads they picked up!

What is the main idea of this paragraph?

_____

_____

3. *Semaphore* is the name for a way of sending messages by flags. The army uses semaphore, and so does the navy. Doctor Albert Myer invented semaphore. The army began to use it in 1858. Doctor Myer credited a Native American tribe for the idea. He got it by watching Comanches in New Mexico signal each other by waving lances.

What is the main idea of this paragraph?

_____

_____

Prewriting

Think of a main idea that you would like to write about, such as your favorite food, a state you would like to visit, or what it would be like to take a trail ride in the desert. Fill in the chart below.

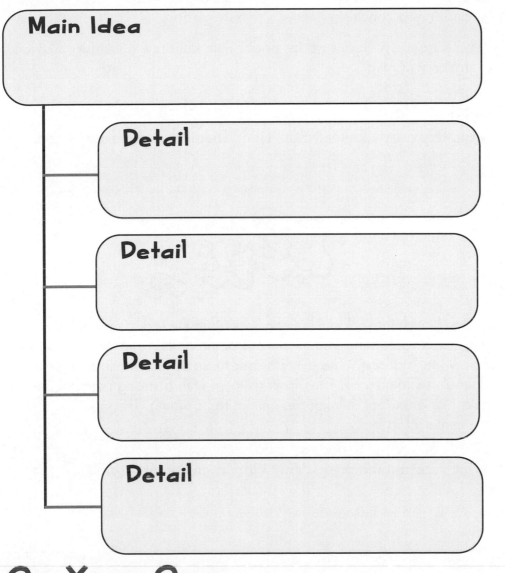

Main Idea

Detail

Detail

Detail

Detail

On Your Own

Now use another sheet of paper to write your paragraph.
Underline the sentence that tells the main idea.

What Is a Conclusion?

A conclusion is a decision you make after thinking about all the information you have. In a story the writer may not state all of his or her ideas. When you read, you often have to hunt for clues so that you can understand the whole story. By putting all of the writer's clues together, you can draw a conclusion about the information.

There are many stories in this book. You will draw conclusions based on the stories you read.

Try It!

Read this story about jellyfish. Think about the information it gives you.

Don't touch that colorful balloon floating in the sea. It's probably a jellyfish. It could sting you. Hundreds of tentacles, or long arms, hang below the "balloon." The jellyfish uses these arms to trap small sea animals swimming by. Then it stings them with a strong poison from its arms. After that, it takes the animal to its mouth. The mouth is at the center of its body.

What conclusion can you draw? Write it on the lines below.

_____

_____

You might have written, "Jellyfish can be very colorful." You might have said, "The poison of the jellyfish can hurt people." You might have written, "The arms of the jellyfish have several uses." You can draw these conclusions from the story. The first sentence compares the jellyfish to a colorful balloon. The next sentences tell what the jellyfish can do with its arms. From these clues you can draw the above conclusions.

Using What You Know

Read the stories on this page. Hunt for clues that will help you draw a conclusion about each school subject being described.

This is my favorite subject. I am learning to read maps. I can tell you what the largest bodies of water are called. I can name the seven continents. I can even tell you what percent of Earth is covered by water.

I am studying _____ .

This subject is a great change of pace during the day. Instead of sitting in a classroom, I go outside and get some exercise. Sometimes I run around the track. Other times I jump over hurdles. If it is raining, I play an indoor game like basketball.

I am studying _____ .

This subject is very important. I study nouns, verbs, and all the parts of speech. I learn to put words together in order to make complete sentences. I am learning how to write well.

I am studying _____ .

This is a fun subject for me because I love to draw. I am able to use pencils, charcoal, and all kinds of paint. I like trying out different colors and designs.

I am studying _____ .

Read each passage. After each passage you will answer a question that will require you to draw a conclusion about the story. Remember, a conclusion is a decision you make after putting together all the clues you are given.

1. Why do people sneeze? Scientists aren't sure why, but they know that sneezing can be a sign of illness. The early Romans believed that sneezing helped people make smart decisions. People in Europe thought that sneezing was a symbol of good health. Any patient who sneezed three times was always released from the hospital.

_____ **1.** From this story you can tell that
   A. sneezing has improved through the years
   B. the early Romans were the first to sneeze
   C. ideas about sneezing have changed over time
   D. most people sneeze only three times

2. People in England used to hold many handwriting contests. The winner usually received a gold pen. In one contest the judges could not decide between two men who wrote beautifully. The judges looked at the handwriting samples for days. They found that one of the men had forgotten to dot an *i*. Because of this the other man walked away with the gold pen.

_____ **2.** One man lost the contest because he
   A. did not want the gold pen
   B. could not write beautifully
   C. forgot an important part of a letter
   D. did not follow the rules of the contest

3. When the United States was new, most people lived on farms. About 95 out of every 100 people made their living by growing food. They ate the food they grew and sold whatever was left over to the people in cities. By 1998, fewer than 3 out of every 100 people were farmers.

_____ **3.** Over time, Americans have been
    A. eating less and less
    B. moving away from farms
    C. moving out of towns and cities
    D. buying more farmland

4. People who visit Washington, D.C., often want souvenirs. Many want a flag that has flown over the dome of the Capitol. To fill these requests, a flag crew takes about 300 flags to the dome every day. They run each flag up the flagpole for a few seconds, and then they take the flag down. The flags are folded, stored, and sold to visitors.

_____ **4.** You can tell from the story that
    A. many flags fly over the Capitol every day
    B. most people cannot tell one flag from another
    C. the flag crew does not like its work
    D. everyone has respect for the American flag

5. A famous poet sat down in a restaurant. A man working in the restaurant recognized the poet. "I will put my poems by the poet's plate," thought the worker. Later the poet read the worker's poems. The next day the worker's name was in the newspapers. His name was Langston Hughes.

_____ **5.** You can conclude that the famous poet
    A. liked the restaurant
    B. did not like the worker's poems
    C. ate pizza
    D. liked the worker's poems

1. Jesse Owens was one of the greatest athletes of the twentieth century. He took part in the 1936 Olympics, in which he won four gold medals. He also won an even greater honor there. That year the Olympics were held in Berlin. The German leader was Adolph Hitler, who believed that white Germans were better than everyone else in the world. Because Owens was an African American, he wanted to prove Hitler wrong. With his great talent, Owens did just that.

_____ **1.** From the story you can tell that
    A. Jesse Owens agreed with Adolph Hitler
    B. Adolph Hitler liked Jesse Owens
    C. Jesse Owens had a special reason for winning
    D. Adolph Hitler was an African American

2. Leslie Silko is a modern writer. She was born in New Mexico. She is part Pueblo, part white, and part Mexican. As a child she heard many Native American stories. She liked the legends of her people. She also learned the customs of her tribe. She uses that knowledge to write stories. She wants everyone to know about the history of Native Americans.

_____ **2.** The story suggests that Leslie Silko
    A. was born in New Jersey
    B. writes about fancy cloth
    C. forgot all her childhood stories
    D. takes pride in her Native American background

3. Pickles are made from cucumbers. People have been eating pickles for more than 4,000 years. People in the United States eat more than 1 billion pounds of pickles each year. There is even a time for celebrating pickles. The third week in May is known as Pickle Week.

_____ **3.** You can tell from the story that
    A. Pickle Week is in March
    B. people in the United States like pickles
    C. pickles are a recent invention
    D. cucumbers are made from pickles

4. A gulf is a body of water that is partly enclosed by land. The Gulf of Mexico is the biggest gulf in the world. It is just south of the United States. This gulf covers 700,000 square miles of Earth's surface. It is 1,000 miles wide from east to west. From north to south, the gulf is 800 miles wide.

_____ **4.** You can conclude that
- **A.** the Gulf of Mexico contains huge amounts of water
- **B.** a gulf is completely surrounded by land
- **C.** the Gulf of Mexico is a river
- **D.** the United States is south of the Gulf of Mexico

5. Checkers is one of the oldest board games. It began in Egypt about 4,000 years ago. It has always been a two-player game, and it has always been played on a checkered board. The game was taken up and changed slightly by the Greeks and the Romans. It soon became a popular game for rich leaders.

_____ **5.** From this story you can conclude that
- **A.** the Greeks and Romans invented checkers
- **B.** checkers is played only by young people
- **C.** only rich leaders should play checkers
- **D.** the Egyptians invented checkers

1. Columns and columns of rock stand along the coast of Ireland. They make up a natural wonder called the Giant's Causeway. An old story says that this bridge was built by a character named Finn MacCool. He was building a bridge so that giants could walk from Ireland to Scotland.

_____ **1.** From this story you can tell that
    A. the causeway must be small
    B. the causeway must be new
    C. MacCool didn't really build the causeway
    D. giants still walk across the causeway

---

2. Many children are familiar with Mother Goose rhymes. Historians aren't sure whether or not Mother Goose was a real person. Some say that her real name was Elizabeth Vergoose. They believe Vergoose is buried in Boston, Massachusetts. Historians think that her son published a book of her songs and rhymes. Such a book has never been found.

_____ **2.** From this story you can tell that
    A. Elizabeth Vergoose wrote a book
    B. the truth about Mother Goose remains a mystery
    C. there was never a real person called Mother Goose
    D. no one tells Mother Goose tales anymore

3. The porcupine uses the quills on its tail to defend itself. When an animal comes too close, the porcupine slaps its tail at the enemy. The sharp quills come off easily. They stick into the other creature's skin. Each quill has a hook at the end. This makes the quills very painful to remove.

_____ **3.** If the quills didn't have hooks, they would
  A. not stay on the porcupine
  B. come out more easily
  C. hurt much more
  D. shoot through the air

---

4. The U.S. Constitution gives people freedom of speech, but that does not mean that people can say whatever they want. What if someone was in a store and wanted to cause trouble? The person could shout, "Fire!" even if there weren't any fire. Everyone would run out of the store at once, and people could get hurt. In this case the guilty person would not be protected under the freedom-of-speech laws.

_____ **4.** You can conclude that the freedom-of-speech laws
  A. are unfair to people
  B. cause trouble in stores
  C. may not protect people who lie
  D. let people say whatever they want

---

5. In the English alphabet, *G* is the seventh letter. It was the third letter in the alphabet of the ancient Greeks. In addition to its main use in forming words, *G* is sometimes used to stand for other words and things. If you are measuring weight, small *g* stands for *gram*. In music, *G* is the name of the note that follows *F*.

_____ **5.** From this story you <u>cannot</u> tell
  A. how to pronounce *G* in English
  B. which things *G* stands for
  C. which place *G* has in the alphabet
  D. what *G* is mainly used for

1. Rosa gave the gift to her friend Maria. It was wrapped in beautiful, handmade paper. She watched as Maria untied the ribbon. Rosa had spent hours making the wrapping paper. In fact she thought the paper was better than the gift. She held her breath as Maria removed the paper and opened the box.

_____ **1.** From this story you can tell that
- **A.** Maria will like the gift
- **B.** Maria will not like the gift
- **C.** Rosa made the greeting card, too
- **D.** Rosa took great care in wrapping the gift

2. In 1987, Lorenzo Amato made a huge pizza. In fact, it was the biggest pizza that had ever been made. It weighed more than 18,000 pounds and was topped with more than 1,000 pounds of cheese. After it was baked, it was cut into 60,000 pieces!

_____ **2.** The story suggests that
- **A.** Amato's pizza fed many people
- **B.** the pizza was not very heavy
- **C.** Amato's pizza tasted awful
- **D.** Amato hated making pizzas

3. Adolfo Esquivel is a great believer in human rights. He lives in Argentina, where he is head of the Peace and Justice Service. This group works hard for the rights of all people. Sometimes the work proves dangerous. For his efforts Esquivel has been jailed and even tortured several times, but he continues his struggle. His work has paid off. He won the Nobel Peace Prize in 1980.

_____ **3.** You can tell from the story that
- **A.** fighting for human rights is always fun
- **B.** Esquivel is willing to suffer for his beliefs
- **C.** Argentina is a state in the United States
- **D.** Esquivel gave up his struggle after being jailed

4. In Czechoslovakia, children celebrate the end of winter in an unusual way. First they make a straw figure. The figure is a symbol of death called Smrt. The straw is decorated with colored rags and bits of eggshell. Then the children burn the straw figure. Sometimes they throw it into a river. After destroying Smrt the children wear flowers to welcome springtime.

_____ **4.** The story suggests that
- **A.** the straw figure is a symbol of summer
- **B.** straw doesn't burn
- **C.** the flowers are a sign of springtime
- **D.** the Czech children hate to see winter end

5. William Taft was once president. He was different in many ways. He was the heaviest president ever. He weighed more than 300 pounds. Taft was the first president to play golf. He was the first one to throw a ball to mark the start of baseball season. Taft died in 1930. He was laid to rest in Arlington National Cemetery. He was the first president to be buried there.

_____ **5.** From the story you can tell that
- **A.** Taft began many presidential customs
- **B.** tennis was Taft's favorite game
- **C.** Taft was a small man
- **D.** President Taft is still alive

1. Juanita was very discouraged about her art. She could hardly draw a tree. One day the art teacher talked to Juanita. "The colors and shapes you use are striking," she said. "I think you have a good chance of winning the art contest this year." The teacher's kind words changed Juanita's attitude.

_____ **1.** This story suggests that
     A. Juanita is not a good artist
     B. color and shape are important art elements
     C. Juanita's teacher cannot draw a tree
     D. Juanita will not enter the art contest

2. Chiang Kai-shek was a famous Chinese leader. As a young man, he gained much power in China. He led the Chinese army against the Japanese in World War II. After the war the Communists tried to take over China. Kai-shek fought bravely against them, but he lost the fight. With his followers he fled to Taiwan. Until his death he continued to fight against the Communist rule of China.

_____ **2.** The story suggests that Chiang Kai-shek
     A. believed that China should remain a free country
     B. is still the leader of China
     C. fled to Japan
     D. was a Communist

3. Seashores experience a daily change in water level. This change is called tide. As the water is pulled from shore, the water level drops. This is known as low tide. As the water returns to shore, the water level rises. This is called high tide. The coming and going of the water is caused by the pull of the Moon's gravity.

_____ **3.** You can tell from the story that
   A. tides are caused by the gravity of the Sun
   B. the water level drops at high tide
   C. the Moon has a strong effect on Earth's seas
   D. a _tide_ is a change in water temperature

---

4. Carbon dioxide in the atmosphere acts as a blanket. It lets light pass through, but it traps heat. This is called the greenhouse effect. It is rather good, for without it Earth would be much colder. As the carbon dioxide increases, the heat of Earth's surface rises. This isn't good. Carbon dioxide comes from the burning of oil, coal, and gasoline. If we do not limit this burning, the world may suffer as a result.

_____ **4.** From this story you can tell that
   A. carbon dioxide traps light
   B. Earth would be warmer without the greenhouse effect
   C. the greenhouse effect is never good
   D. too much carbon dioxide is bad

---

5. Have you ever looked up a word in a dictionary? Well, you can thank Noah Webster. He worked almost all his life to make spelling fit a standard in America. He produced two large books of words. The larger one appeared in 1828. Webster's work has been improved many times. His dictionary is still in use today.

_____ **5.** You can conclude that Noah Webster
   A. respected and loved language
   B. didn't know how to spell
   C. liked to write long letters
   D. couldn't read

1. Many cities hold distance races called marathons. Runners gather from around the country. They race through the streets, up and down hills, and over bridges. People who want something different can go run a marathon in Indiana. The runners there dash down the dark passages of the Merengo Cave!

_____ **1.** From this story you can tell that
   A. all marathons are alike
   B. most runners like cave races
   C. Merengo Cave must be pretty long
   D. marathons are bicycle races

2. Moths are related to butterflies. However, most moths fly at night. Butterflies fly during the day. When a moth is resting, it folds its wings back over its body. A butterfly, on the other hand, holds its wings upward.

_____ **2.** This story tells
   A. how moths and butterflies are alike
   B. how moths and butterflies are different
   C. why people confuse moths and butterflies
   D. why moths are better than butterflies

3. The sidewinder is a snake that lives in the desert. Unlike other snakes the sidewinder does not crawl. Instead, it coils its body into big loops. Then suddenly it unwinds itself. The snake skims over the sand much like a leaf in the wind. It moves forward and slightly sideways at the same time.

_____ **3.** The sidewinder gets its name from
   A. the place in which it lives
   B. the way in which it moves
   C. the fact that it moves easily
   D. a group of other snakes

4. Inventors record their inventions with the government. The inventors hope that someone will buy their bright ideas. Some inventions are so strange that no one wants them. Government files show inventions for odd things, such as flying fire escapes and eyeglasses for chickens. There is even an alarm clock that taps the sleeping person on the head with a piece of wood!

_____ **4.** The story tells about inventions that
    A. do not work
    B. were turned down by the government
    C. have been used in many places
    D. no one wants to buy

5. White eggs and brown eggs taste exactly the same. In some places, however, people think that brown eggs are better. They are willing to pay more money for them. For example, in Boston brown eggs usually cost more than they do in New York.

_____ **5.** You could conclude that people in New York
    A. don't eat brown eggs
    B. think brown eggs are best
    C. eat more eggs than people eat in Boston
    D. don't think brown eggs are better

1. Some people love a good story. Once every year a group of people get together for a storytelling festival. They take turns entertaining each other by spinning yarns and swapping tales.

_____ **1.** You can tell that
    A. storytellers like wool
    B. the festival has many activities
    C. the festival is dull
    D. storytellers like to share stories

2. By noting changes, a lie-detector machine shows whether someone is lying. The machine shows changes in heartbeat and breathing. These changes might take place when a person is lying. These changes also take place when a person is nervous. Sometimes a person is lying but doesn't know it. In this case the machine doesn't note any change at all.

_____ **2.** From the story you <u>cannot</u> tell
    A. what happens when a person lies
    B. what a lie detector shows
    C. which changes take place when a person is nervous
    D. how a lie detector is used in court

3. In the making of a baseball, machines do most of the work. One machine covers a piece of cork with rubber. Another machine wraps yarn around the ball. The leather used to cover the ball is also cut by a machine. People are still needed to sew the leather covers on the balls by hand.

_____ **3.** You can tell that machines
   A. probably can't sew leather covers on balls
   B. always get tangled up in the yarn
   C. make the cork used for making balls
   D. can't cover cork with rubber

---

4. The United States once had a state named for Benjamin Franklin. It was at the time that North Carolina gave some land to the new government. The land was later returned to North Carolina. Today that land is part of the state of Tennessee.

_____ **4.** From the story you <u>cannot</u> tell
   A. who Benjamin Franklin was
   B. where the state was located
   C. when we had a state named for Franklin
   D. what happened to the state

---

5. Many animals shed their outer coverings every year. Then they grow new ones. Birds lose their feathers and grow new, colorful ones. Snakes lose their old skins. New, shiny skin forms underneath the old skin. Some mammals lose part of their hair in warm weather. They grow heavy coats in cold weather.

_____ **5.** Some mammals lose part of their hair
   A. so that they can grow larger
   B. in order to keep cool
   C. when cold weather is on the way
   D. when they are babies

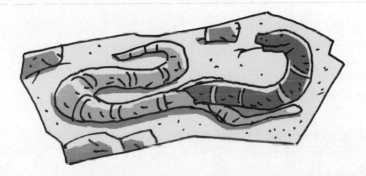

1. The man carefully eyed the painting in the flea market. The picture was torn, but the frame was in good shape. The man decided to pay the asking price of $4. Later when the man removed the picture from the frame, he found an old piece of paper. The man's eyes widened in surprise because he had found an old copy of the Declaration of Independence. It was worth $1 million!

_____ **1.** You can conclude that
   A. the man always had rotten luck
   B. the old piece of paper was a restaurant menu
   C. the man was glad that he bought the painting
   D. the frame was worth $1 million

2. Mary Bacon loved to ride horses, and she turned that love into a job. Being one of the first female jockeys, Mary rode her horses to many wins, but she also experienced many setbacks. One time she was thrown from a horse and broke her back. Another time a horse fell on top of her. Each time she returned to race again. She once said, "You can't quit just because you've been thrown."

_____ **2.** From the story you <u>cannot</u> tell
   A. about Bacon's job
   B. which horse threw Bacon in 1969
   C. if Bacon returned to racing after her accidents
   D. how Bacon broke her back

3. Charles Edensaw was a member of the Haida tribe. He lived in western Canada. Edensaw became a fine artist. He used wood, gold, and silver in his works. He was also a talented crafter of argillite, which is a kind of shale. His art included drawings, sketches, pipes, and totem poles. Many of his works are found in museums.

_____ **3.** From this story you can tell that
   A. Charles Edensaw was a successful artist
   B. all of Edensaw's works are missing today
   C. Edensaw used only crayons in his works
   D. the Haida tribe lived in Kansas

4. Sonja Henie was one of the best ice-skaters of all time. Her first major contest was the 1924 Winter Olympics. Henie was just 12 years old! She won gold medals in the next three Olympics. She even won 10 world titles in a row. Then Henie became a movie star. Her movies often showed her skating. As a result, ice-skating was soon a popular sport around the world.

_____ **4.** From the story you <u>cannot</u> tell
  A. which sport Henie was best at
  B. how many movies Henie made
  C. when Henie's first major contest took place
  D. how many world titles Henie won in a row

5. Estella was looking at ruby rings. She knew that the stone had special meaning, for it was considered the birthstone for July. That was why Estella thought she should have one. Estella had a pearl ring, but she did not have a ruby ring. She hoped that someone would get one for her for her birthday.

_____ **5.** You can conclude from the story that
  A. Estella does not really like rubies
  B. rubies cost a lot of money
  C. the rings Estella saw were made of gold
  D. Estella's birthday is in July

Writing Roundup

Read each paragraph. Think about a conclusion you can draw. Write your conclusion in a complete sentence.

1. Jumping from a plane is a daring act. Imagine how daring it would be if you were the first to do it. Georgia Broadwick was such a person. On June 21, 1913, she jumped from a plane over Los Angeles. She fell 100 feet before her parachute opened. She was the first woman to parachute from a plane. In those days, just going up in a plane was daring enough!

What conclusion can you draw from this paragraph?

_____

_____

2. Have you ever seen a $100,000 bill? These bills were made in 1935. They had a portrait of Woodrow Wilson on them. The bills were not put into public use. They were used only by the government.

What conclusion can you draw from this paragraph?

_____

_____

3. Amalia does not remember who taught her to whistle. She does remember the first bird she learned how to imitate. It was a robin. Since then, Amalia has learned to make the sounds of many birds.

What conclusion can you draw from this paragraph?

_____

_____

Read the paragraph below. What conclusions can you draw? Use the clues in the paragraph to answer the questions in complete sentences.

Jackie Robinson was the first African American to play major-league baseball. He joined the Brooklyn Dodgers in 1947. Another African American joined the Dodgers team later that year. His name was Dan Bankhead. He pitched in four games. He also hit a home run. The next year Bankhead returned to the minor leagues. Robinson was voted into the Baseball Hall of Fame. Still, Bankhead should not be forgotten. It took courage for him to play with the Dodgers in 1947.

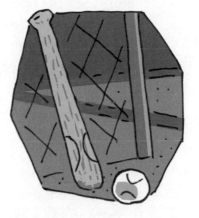

1. Did any African Americans play in the major leagues in 1946? How do you know?

_____

_____

2. In Jackie Robinson's first game with the Dodgers, was he the only African American in the major leagues? How do you know?

_____

_____

3. Was Dan Bankhead a star with the Dodgers? How do you know?

_____

_____

4. Was Jackie Robinson a baseball star? How do you know?

_____

_____

unit 6

What Is an Inference?

An inference is a guess you make after thinking about what you already know. Suppose you are going to the post office. From what you know about the post office, you might infer that you will wait in line at the counter. You can assume that when it is your turn, you will pay the fee for the services you need.

An author does not write every detail in a story. If every detail were included, stories would be long and boring, and the main point would be lost. Suppose an author wrote, "Debra ran along the beach." The writer does not have to tell you what a beach is. You already know that it is a sandy area next to the ocean. From what you know, you might guess that people who go to the beach can swim, build sand castles, or collect seashells. By filling in these missing details, you could infer that Debra was at the beach to swim in the waves with her family. You can infer the missing details from what you know.

Try It!

Read this story about foxes. Think about the facts.

Foxes sleep during the day and hunt at night. They prey on squirrels, rabbits, frogs, and birds. They also eat eggs and berries. Although foxes often live near people, they usually stay hidden. If a person approaches them, they will run away or climb up a tree.

What inference can you make about foxes? Write an inference on the line below.

_____

You might have written something such as: "Foxes are afraid of people." You can make this inference from what the story tells you and what you already know. You know that if an animal hides or runs away, it is not comfortable around people.

Practice Making Inferences

Read each story. Then read the statements that follow. Some of the statements are facts and can be found in the story. Other statements are inferences. You can make these by thinking about what you've read and what you know. Decide whether each statement is a fact or an inference. The first one has been done for you.

Laura had $5.00. Her mother had given the money to her so that she could buy a present for her brother. While Laura was shopping, she saw a book she had been wanting to read. It cost $4.50.

Fact	Inference	
●	○	**1. A.** Laura had $5.00.
●	○	**B.** The book cost $4.50.
○	●	**C.** Laura bought the book she wanted.
○	●	**D.** She didn't have a present to give to her brother.

You can find statements **A** and **B** in the story. They are facts. You can infer that Laura bought the book and that she didn't have a present to give to her brother, but this is not stated in the story. Statements **c** and **D** are inferences.

Juan lives in Madrid, Spain. He teaches at a private school. Juan walks to work every weekday and holds classes from 9:00 until noon. Then he walks home for lunch. His family eats a large meal, and then everyone takes a nap. Juan returns to work at 4:00 and teaches until 9:00 at night.

Fact	Inference	
○	○	**2. A.** Juan teaches at a private school.
○	○	**B.** He walks to work every weekday.
○	○	**C.** Juan's family feels drowsy after lunch.
○	○	**D.** The school is near Juan's home.

Read the passages. Use what you know about inference to answer the questions. Remember, an inference is a guess you make by putting together what you know and what you read or see in the stories.

1. The Lincoln Highway opened in 1913. It was the first paved road in the United States that stretched from coast to coast. The highway started at Times Square in New York City. It ran more than 3,000 miles to California. There it reached its end at Lincoln Park in San Francisco.

Fact	Inference		
○	○	**1. A.**	The Lincoln Highway opened in 1913.
○	○	**B.**	Many people drove on the new highway.
○	○	**C.**	The road made cross-country travel easier.
○	○	**D.**	The highway was more than 3,000 miles long.

2. Sometimes the Moon passes between the Earth and the Sun and completely blocks the Sun's light. On Earth it looks as if the Sun has disappeared. This is called a total solar eclipse. Stars appear in the sky. Flowers close their petals. Many animals are fooled into going to sleep. As the Moon continues to move, the Sun can be seen again. First it appears as a tiny sliver, then a crescent, then the full Sun. Roosters begin to crow and flowers open back up. Long ago people were afraid that the Sun had been swallowed by a monster. They would beat drums to scare the monster away. Now we know that total solar eclipses happen every 18 months or so. They last just a few minutes. Each eclipse can be seen only from certain places on Earth.

Fact	Inference		
○	○	**2. A.**	People used to be afraid that the Sun would not reappear.
○	○	**B.**	A total solar eclipse is visible only from certain parts of Earth.
○	○	**C.**	During an eclipse it is possible to see the stars.
○	○	**D.**	A total solar eclipse lasts only a few minutes.

3. Elizabeth Butler was an English painter. She enjoyed painting battle scenes. Butler often worked on a very large canvas in order to capture the whole scene. Her paintings are full of life and interest. Her most famous painting is named *The Roll Call*.

Fact	Inference	
○	○	**3. A.** Elizabeth Butler was a painter.
○	○	**B.** Butler felt battle scenes were exciting.
○	○	**C.** One of Butler's paintings is *The Roll Call*.
○	○	**D.** Butler visited battle scenes to get ideas.

---

4. Harvest moon is a full moon that comes in late September or early October. At this time of year, the Moon rises slowly. It seems to hang near the horizon for a long time after sunset. Because of this the Moon reflects more light from the Sun. The twilight is brighter, and farmers have extra time to harvest their crops.

Fact	Inference	
○	○	**4. A.** Farmers can't harvest crops in the dark.
○	○	**B.** The Moon reflects the Sun's light.
○	○	**C.** Farmers like the harvest moon.
○	○	**D.** The harvest moon is a full moon.

---

5. The New York Yankees play baseball in Yankee Stadium. This ballpark opened in 1923. More than 70,000 people crowded in on opening day. They all wanted to see the Yankees play in the new park. That day Babe Ruth hit a home run. It was the first ball hit out of Yankee Stadium.

Fact	Inference	
○	○	**5. A.** In 1923 baseball was popular in New York.
○	○	**B.** Yankee Stadium is in New York.
○	○	**C.** Babe Ruth hit a home run on opening day.
○	○	**D.** Yankee Stadium opened in 1923.

1. Some animals make long journeys to escape cold or to find food. For example, a gray whale can travel up to 5,600 miles. Bats have been known to travel as far as 1,500 miles, and the record distance traveled by a butterfly is 4,000 miles. For toads the record is 2 miles. This may not seem like much, but that's a lot of hopping!

Fact	Inference		
○	○	**1.** **A.**	A butterfly has traveled 4,000 miles.
○	○	**B.**	Some animals travel to escape cold.
○	○	**C.**	Scientists can track how far an animal travels.
○	○	**D.**	Some bats have traveled 1,500 miles.

2. The date was January 10, 1901. Captain Anthony Lucas had his men hard at work in the Spindletop oil field in Texas. Suddenly their equipment began to shake. Then oil gushed from the ground, shooting high into the air. Everything nearby was coated with the thick, black oil. Lucas and his men didn't mind, because they had struck oil! Spindletop soon became one of the highest-producing oil fields in the world.

Fact	Inference		
○	○	**2.** **A.**	The Spindletop oil field was in Texas.
○	○	**B.**	Captain Lucas knew a lot about oil wells.
○	○	**C.**	Lucas and his men found oil.
○	○	**D.**	It was exciting when the men struck oil.

3. Have you ever been in a hailstorm? The balls of ice can cause great damage. A hailstone begins as a raindrop that is blown high up into a thundercloud, where it freezes. The lump of ice is blown back up several times, each time gaining more ice. Finally it grows too heavy and falls to Earth.

Fact	Inference		
○	○	**3.** **A.**	Hail can be dangerous.
○	○	**B.**	A hailstone begins as a raindrop.
○	○	**C.**	Winds blow the lump of ice back up.
○	○	**D.**	Hail falls when it grows too heavy.

4. Have you ever heard of a "swan song"? This saying means a farewell appearance or a final act. The saying comes from an ancient legend about swans. It was once thought that a swan would remain silent all its life until it was dying. Then it would sing out in its final minutes. This swan song would be one of great feeling and beauty.

Fact	Inference		
◯	◯	**4. A.**	Ancient people thought swans were special.
◯	◯	**B.**	A "swan song" means a final act.
◯	◯	**C.**	Swans were supposedly silent until near death.
◯	◯	**D.**	The swan's final song was supposed to be very beautiful.

---

5. Before 1892, women did not play basketball. Senda Berenson started women's basketball. Many people thought that women should not play sports as rough as basketball. Berenson changed the rules a little to make the game more "ladylike." However, women soon began playing the game just like men.

Fact	Inference		
◯	◯	**5. A.**	Berenson changed some of the rules.
◯	◯	**B.**	Many people thought that women should not play basketball.
◯	◯	**C.**	Women's basketball began in 1892.
◯	◯	**D.**	Some people did not like women's basketball.

1. Krakatoa was an island in the Indian Ocean. It lay just west of Java. On the island was a large volcano. In 1883, the volcano blew up. The whole island was destroyed. The noise of the blast was heard thousands of miles away. The blast also formed a giant wave more that 100 feet tall. The wave swept over nearby islands and killed 40,000 people. Ash from the volcano darkened the region for two days. Dust reached the atmosphere and spread over the whole Earth.

Fact   Inference

○   ○   **1. A.** Krakatoa was in the Indian Ocean.

○   ○   **B.** The volcano blew up in 1883.

○   ○   **C.** Every person on Krakatoa was killed.

○   ○   **D.** The giant wave killed 40,000 people.

---

2. The bell rang sharply in the middle of the night. Missy sat upright in her bed, rubbing her eyes. Again the sharp ringing split the silence. Trying to pull herself together, Missy scrambled for the phone. She had no idea who could be calling at that time of night, but she hoped it was not an emergency. When she answered the phone, a voice at the other end asked for someone named Felix. Disgusted, Missy said that Felix did not live there. Then the person on the other end slammed down the phone.

Fact   Inference

○   ○   **2. A.** Missy was asleep when the phone rang.

○   ○   **B.** The other person dialed a wrong number.

○   ○   **C.** The phone rang in the middle of the night.

○   ○   **D.** The other person did not apologize.

3. In July 1969, a spaceship rushed toward the Moon. The ship was called *Apollo 11*. On board were three men. They were Michael Collins, Neil Armstrong, and Edwin Aldrin Jr. When the spaceship neared the Moon, it began to orbit. Then a smaller craft carried two men to the Moon's surface. Neil Armstrong became the first man to walk on the Moon. He was soon followed by Edwin Aldrin Jr.

Fact	Inference		
○	○	**3. A.**	*Apollo 11* went to the Moon.
○	○	**B.**	Three men were on *Apollo 11*.
○	○	**C.**	Armstrong was the first to walk on the Moon.
○	○	**D.**	Collins remained on the spaceship.

4. *Dandelion* was first a French word. It refers to a part of a lion. Long ago the flower was called "lion's tooth" because of the leaf's shape. In French it was known as *dent de lion*, or tooth of the lion. After a while this became the English word *dandelion*.

Fact	Inference		
○	○	**4. A.**	*Dandelion* comes from a French word.
○	○	**B.**	In French the name meant "lion's tooth."
○	○	**C.**	Dandelions grow in France.
○	○	**D.**	People thought the leaf looked like a tooth.

5. Lewis Carroll was a successful British writer. His real name was Charles Dodgson. He wrote about a small girl named Alice. Perhaps you have read his book called *Alice's Adventures in Wonderland*.

Fact	Inference		
○	○	**5. A.**	Carroll was a successful writer.
○	○	**B.**	Charles Dodgson was Carroll's real name.
○	○	**C.**	Carroll wrote about a girl named Alice.
○	○	**D.**	*Alice's Adventures in Wonderland* is a popular book.

1. Mei came to the United States from China when she was two years old. She was adopted by American parents. When she turned 12 years old, her parents took her to China to visit her uncle. Mei learned much about the Chinese culture. From then on, Mei visited China every year. She felt lucky to have family in two different countries.

Fact	Inference		
○	○	**1.** **A.**	Mei lived in China before she moved to America.
○	○	**B.**	Mei visited her uncle in China.
○	○	**C.**	Mei loved the Chinese culture.
○	○	**D.**	Mei was glad that American parents adopted her.

2. Jakob and Wilhelm Grimm lived in Germany. They loved many of the folktales told in their country. The brothers collected the tales and published them in a book. Now many people know of *Grimm's Fairy Tales*. The collection has been translated into many different languages.

Fact	Inference		
○	○	**2.** **A.**	The Grimm brothers lived in Germany.
○	○	**B.**	The folktales were first told in German.
○	○	**C.**	The brothers loved many German folktales.
○	○	**D.**	People in many parts of the world like folktales.

3. Drive-in movies were once a fun family outing. The whole gang would pile into the car and head to the drive-in. Beneath the stars they would munch popcorn and watch a movie. The first drive-in movie opened in New Jersey in 1933. Now there are only a few drive-in movies left.

Fact	Inference		
○	○	**3.** **A.**	Drive-in movies were popular in the past.
○	○	**B.**	The first drive-in movie was in New Jersey.
○	○	**C.**	People don't go to drive-in movies much now.
○	○	**D.**	The first drive-in opened in 1933.

4. Delbert had planned a big party for Saturday. He invited many of his friends from school and even a few old friends from across town. He bought some tasty refreshments and picked out some good music. When the time of the party arrived, the doorbell did not ring. An hour later, as Delbert sat alone munching corn chips in his living room, there was a knock on his door.

Fact	Inference	
○	○	**4. A.** Delbert picked out some good music.
○	○	**B.** He expected his friends to come to the party.
○	○	**C.** Delbert's friends were late to the party.
○	○	**D.** Delbert ate his corn chips alone.

---

5. Vampire bats almost never bite humans. Movies have made people think that vampire bats hurt us, but movies are not real. Vampire bats usually bite sleeping cows and then lick up a tiny amount of blood from the wound. The bite is so small and harmless that it does not even wake up the cow. Since vampire bats are wild, some of them may get rabies. Only vampire bats that carry rabies are dangerous.

Fact	Inference	
○	○	**5. A.** Healthy vampire bats do not hurt cows.
○	○	**B.** Vampire bats with rabies are dangerous.
○	○	**C.** Some movies do not tell the truth about bats.
○	○	**D.** Vampire bats usually bite cattle.

1. "A package came for you today," Greg's mother said as he walked in. "I think it's from Aunt Ginny." Greg peeled the tape from the box and ripped off the brown paper. He tore off the gift wrap to find a stuffed bear inside. Aunt Ginny never seemed to realize that he was no longer three years old and hadn't been for more than seven years. Then he thought about the trouble Aunt Ginny had gone through to select the present and mail it. Greg sat down at the kitchen table with a pen and paper.

Fact	Inference	
○	○	**1. A.** The present was a stuffed bear.
○	○	**B.** Greg did not like the gift.
○	○	**C.** His aunt doesn't see Greg very often.
○	○	**D.** Greg is a thoughtful boy.

2. Meg was dyeing a T-shirt for a friend. Her 18-month-old sister Sue was watching. Sue was very interested in the process. Meg filled a big plastic tub with dye. When Meg left the room to get a bucket of water, Sue grabbed onto the wobbly sides of the tub and pulled herself up to look inside.

Fact	Inference	
○	○	**2. A.** Sue was curious.
○	○	**B.** Meg was dyeing a shirt.
○	○	**C.** By leaving Sue alone, Meg acted carelessly.
○	○	**D.** Sue pulled the tub over.

3. The ostrich is the largest bird in the world. It can grow to more than 9 feet tall. Although ostriches cannot fly, these African birds can run quite fast. Their highest speed is about 40 miles per hour. Ostrich eggs are very large and weigh about 4 pounds. That's 24 times as heavy as a chicken egg!

Fact	Inference	
◯	◯	**3.** **A.** Chicken eggs are much smaller than ostrich eggs.
◯	◯	**B.** Ostriches cannot fly.
◯	◯	**C.** Nine feet high is very tall for a bird.
◯	◯	**D.** Ostriches can run up to 40 miles per hour.

4. The nursery rhyme "Humpty Dumpty" might have been written about King Richard III of England. The king had a horse named Wall. When King Richard lost an important battle, he lost his position as king. It is perhaps this event that the rhyme talks about in the line "Humpty Dumpty had a great fall."

Fact	Inference	
◯	◯	**4.** **A.** "Humpty Dumpty" is a rhyme.
◯	◯	**B.** It was important for kings to win in battle.
◯	◯	**C.** King Richard III had a horse named Wall.
◯	◯	**D.** Richard III was once the king of England.

5. Burt had played the saxophone for three years. This year he got up the courage to try out for the jazz band. For weeks before the tryout, he practiced every day after school for an hour. On the day of the tryout, he was very nervous and did not do well. When he found out he did not make the jazz band, he was very disappointed. A few weeks later, the music teacher decided another sax was needed, and she asked Burt to join the jazz band.

Fact	Inference	
◯	◯	**5.** **A.** Burt really wanted to be in the jazz band.
◯	◯	**B.** Burt plays the saxophone.
◯	◯	**C.** Burt was disappointed about not being chosen.
◯	◯	**D.** The teacher asked Burt to join the band.

1. Crocodiles lay their eggs in sand. Three months later the eggs are ready to hatch. The baby crocodiles are too weak to dig out of the sand around them, so they start to peep from inside their shells. Their mother, who has never strayed very far away, hears the calls and digs the eggs out.

Fact	Inference	
○	○	**1. A.** The mother stays nearby so she can hear the babies.
○	○	**B.** The babies have loud voices.
○	○	**C.** Sand protects the crocodile eggs.
○	○	**D.** The mother digs the eggs out.

2. Stuart always did very well on science tests, but his friend Kevin had trouble with science. Next week's test on the planets seemed especially difficult to Kevin. The Saturday before the test, Kevin asked Stuart if he would help him study. Although Stuart had planned to play soccer with his friends that afternoon, he decided to change his plans and help Kevin instead.

Fact	Inference	
○	○	**2. A.** Kevin has trouble with science.
○	○	**B.** Stuart changed his plans.
○	○	**C.** Kevin wanted to make better science grades.
○	○	**D.** Stuart is a kind friend.

3. Have you ever thought about how keys open doors? A key is cut a special way so that it matches the pattern of its lock. Inside the lock there is a metal bar. A row of pins holds the bar in place. When the matching key is put into the lock, it raises the pins and allows the bar to move. The bar then slides out of the way and unlocks the door when the key is turned.

Fact	Inference	
○	○	**3. A.** Keys are cut a special way.
○	○	**B.** A metal bar is inside the lock.
○	○	**C.** The bar keeps the door locked.
○	○	**D.** The wrong key won't raise a lock's pins.

4. Although Duke was a dog, the Clark family treated him like a member of the family. They took Duke everywhere with them, even on vacation. Once, on their way home from the mountains, they stopped at a rest area after several hours of driving. Ten minutes later everyone piled into the van to continue the trip. Since they were in a hurry to get home, no one checked to make sure Duke was with them.

Fact	Inference	
○	○	**4.** **A.** The Clarks loved their dog.
○	○	**B.** Duke went everywhere with the Clarks.
○	○	**C.** The Clarks treated Duke like a family member.
○	○	**D.** Duke was left behind at the rest area.

5. Ruth's hobby was making radio-controlled airplanes. But even more than making them, she enjoyed flying the planes. Once Ruth spent every weekend for an entire month working with her dad to build an airplane. The next Saturday Ruth decided to try out the plane. When Ruth set up the airplane for takeoff, she didn't notice the tall pine trees standing in its path.

Fact	Inference	
○	○	**5.** **A.** Ruth enjoys flying radio-controlled planes.
○	○	**B.** Tall trees were in the path of the plane.
○	○	**C.** The airplane crashed in the trees.
○	○	**D.** Ruth worked with her dad to build a plane.

1. When she was a girl, Marian Anderson dreamed of becoming a famous concert singer. In those days, that dream seemed impossible for someone who was both poor and black. When she was 17, she began studying with a famous voice teacher. Within a year she performed throughout the South in her first concert tour. In the 1930s she sang all over the world. In 1963, President Lyndon Johnson awarded her the Presidential Medal of Freedom.

Fact	Inference		
○	○	1. **A.**	Anderson was a talented singer.
○	○	**B.**	A famous teacher gave Anderson lessons.
○	○	**C.**	Anderson was respected by many people.
○	○	**D.**	President Johnson gave Anderson an award.

2. Dean was five years old. He couldn't tie his shoes yet, and they were almost always untied. One day his sister Nancy decided to help him learn to tie his shoes. The first step was easy for him, but he had trouble with the loop. Nancy worked with him patiently for three days. On the third day, Dean proudly showed his parents how he could tie his shoes.

Fact	Inference		
○	○	2. **A.**	Dean's shoes were often untied.
○	○	**B.**	Nancy is a patient person.
○	○	**C.**	Dean's parents were proud of him.
○	○	**D.**	Nancy helped Dean learn to tie his shoes.

3. Camels do not need much water. During the cool months in the desert, they usually do not drink water since they get enough from the plants they eat. When the temperature is around 95 degrees, they can go about 15 days without a drink. When the temperature is 104 degrees, camels drink water whenever they can.

Fact	Inference		
◯	◯	**3. A.**	Camels need more water in hotter weather.
◯	◯	**B.**	Camels can go 15 days without a drink.
◯	◯	**C.**	Eating plants provides camels with water.
◯	◯	**D.**	Camels are used to living in dry climates.

4. Patty and her mom were very excited to plant their first garden. They looked forward to growing their own vegetables. First they used a hoe to prepare the soil. Then they added peat moss to the soil. They planted tomatoes, lettuce, beans, and peas. Every week Patty spent at least an hour weeding and watering the plants. At the end of the summer, Patty shared the vegetables with her friends.

Fact	Inference		
◯	◯	**4. A.**	Patty planted tomatoes in her garden.
◯	◯	**B.**	They prepared the soil with a hoe.
◯	◯	**C.**	Her friends appreciated the vegetables.
◯	◯	**D.**	Patty is a hard worker.

5. Lightning was the cause of many house fires before lightning rods became popular. Lightning rods can prevent such disasters. In 1753, Benjamin Franklin published instructions for making lightning rods. Soon afterwards women in Europe started wearing lightning rods on their hats.

Fact	Inference		
◯	◯	**5. A.**	Hats were in fashion during the 1750s.
◯	◯	**B.**	European women were afraid of lightning.
◯	◯	**C.**	Lightning rods can prevent house fires.
◯	◯	**D.**	Many house fires were caused by lightning.

1. The first pair of roller skates was made in 1760 by Joseph Merlin. Merlin tried to sell his skates in London, but he didn't have much success. One problem was that they didn't have brakes! That problem was soon solved, and more people began trying the new sport. Roller skating became more popular as the result of a play staged in 1849. The actors were supposed to ice skate, but they could not make ice on stage. So the actors used roller skates instead.

Fact	Inference	
○	○	**1. A.** A play made roller skating more popular.
○	○	**B.** At first roller skates were not popular.
○	○	**C.** Merlin made the first roller skates.
○	○	**D.** Skates were dangerous without brakes.

2. John was out of school, and he wished he had something to do. One morning he read in the newspaper that volunteers were needed at the local hospital. That afternoon John called the hospital and offered to help three days a week.

Fact	Inference	
○	○	**2. A.** John was on summer vacation.
○	○	**B.** John was bored.
○	○	**C.** John offered to help.
○	○	**D.** John likes to help people.

3. Charlie Chaplin was one of the first movie actors. Americans loved "The Little Tramp" from London, who lived in the United States. In Chaplin's later movies, he gave his opinions about the United States government. When he left the United States for a vacation, the government would not let him enter the country again. Twenty-three years later, after he was finally allowed to return to the United States, the queen of England made him a knight.

Fact	Inference	
○	○	**3. A.** "The Little Tramp" was Chaplin's nickname.
○	○	**B.** Chaplin was made a knight.
○	○	**C.** The queen enjoyed Chaplin's movies.
○	○	**D.** Chaplin disagreed with the United States government.

4. In some parts of the country in the 1880s, soda fountain owners were not allowed to serve sodas on Sundays. Illinois owners got around the law by serving the syrup on ice cream rather than with fizzy water. The new idea was called a "Sunday soda." The dish later became known as a sundae.

Fact	Inference		
○	○	**4. A.**	Soda fountains were open on Sundays.
○	○	**B.**	Customers liked the "Sunday sodas."
○	○	**C.**	Sodas are made only with syrup and fizzy water.
○	○	**D.**	The dish became known as a sundae.

---

5. Rhonda was walking 10 miles to raise money for a new cancer center. It was 90 degrees that day, and some of her friends had dropped out after the sixth mile. Now Rhonda was in the final mile, and her throat was dry. As she looked ahead, Rhonda saw her father holding a tall glass of lemonade.

Fact	Inference		
○	○	**5. A.**	Rhonda didn't want to give up.
○	○	**B.**	It was a 90-degree day.
○	○	**C.**	Rhonda's friends dropped out of the race.
○	○	**D.**	Rhonda felt better when she saw her father.

Writing Roundup

Read each story. Then read the question that follows it. Write your answers on the lines below each question.

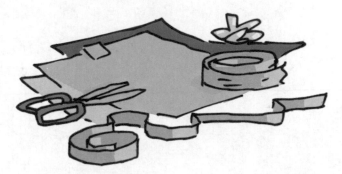

1. Carmela opened the brightly colored paper and spread it across the table. Then she positioned the box on the paper. It fit nicely. Next she neatly folded the paper and taped it into place. This was going to be a pleasant surprise for her mother, but it would be better if Carmela could find a bow.

What was Carmela doing?

_____

_____

2. A few green leaves were left on the tree, but they didn't look very good. The tree bark looked bad, too. The sun was shining bright, but this tree needed something else.

What was wrong with the tree?

_____

_____

3. Yoko didn't realize that there were so many different stamps. She didn't know which ones and how many she would need for a letter to her cousin. She could ask when she went to the counter.

Where was Yoko?

_____

_____

Read the paragraph below. Then answer the questions.

The Sun was setting when Bernardo got off his ladder. He had another bucket of cherries to add to his picking for the day. To Bernardo, the picking of cherries was the easiest work on his farm, but after 12 hours, his fingers and arms ached. They had a right to be aching. After all, they'd been working his farm for 40 years. Bernardo had been almost 30 years old when he purchased the farm. He'd believed his children would take over at some time, but they had gone off once they finished school. Now Bernardo was all alone, and keeping up the farm was a struggle.

1. How old is Bernardo?

_____

_____

2. Why did Bernardo need a ladder?

_____

_____

3. What kind of person is Bernardo?

_____

_____

4. Why was keeping up the farm such a struggle for Bernardo?

_____

_____

Check Yourself

Unit 1

What Are Facts?

p. 6

Fact: There are more than 2,400 different kinds of snakes.

Fact: One of the smallest snakes is the thread snake.

Practice Finding Facts

p. 7

3. A

LESSON 1 pp. 8–9
1. C   6. D
2. B   7. B
3. A   8. A
4. C   9. C
5. B   10. B

LESSON 2 pp. 10–11
1. C   6. C
2. A   7. D
3. D   8. A
4. B   9. B
5. D   10. A

LESSON 3 pp. 12–13
1. C   6. D
2. D   7. C
3. A   8. A
4. B   9. D
5. D   10. A

LESSON 4 pp. 14–15
1. C   6. A
2. B   7. C
3. D   8. B
4. A   9. C
5. C   10. C

LESSON 5 pp. 16–17
1. C   6. C
2. A   7. A
3. D   8. B
4. A   9. C
5. B   10. D

LESSON 6 pp. 18–19
1. B   6. D
2. C   7. A
3. D   8. B
4. B   9. B
5. C   10. B

LESSON 7 pp. 20–21
1. B   6. B
2. C   7. A
3. C   8. D
4. A   9. C
5. B   10. C

LESSON 8 pp. 22–23
1. A   6. D
2. B   7. C
3. C   8. D
4. B   9. A
5. C   10. B

Writing Roundup

p. 24

Possible answers include:

1. In ancient times salt was often traded for gold.

2. "You are worth your salt" means you are worth the money you are being paid.

3. Salty water is called brine.

p. 25

Check that you have four facts in your paragraph.

Unit 2

What Is Sequence?

p. 26

2, 3, 1

Practice with Sequence

p. 27

3. B

LESSON 1 pp. 28–29
1. 3, 1, 2
2. B
3. A
4. C
5. B

LESSON 2 pp. 30–31
1. 2, 3, 1
2. B
3. A
4. C
5. C

LESSON 3 pp. 32–33
1. 3, 2, 1
2. C
3. B
4. A
5. B

LESSON 4 pp. 34–35
1. 3, 2, 1
2. A
3. C
4. C
5. C

LESSON 5 pp. 36–37
1. 1, 2, 3
2. C
3. B
4. A
5. C

LESSON 6 pp. 38–39
1. 1, 3, 2
2. C
3. A
4. B
5. C

LESSON 7 pp. 40–41
1. 2, 1, 3
2. B
3. B
4. C
5. A

LESSON 8 pp. 42–43
1. 3, 2, 1
2. C
3. A
4. B
5. C

Writing Roundup

p. 44

Possible answers include:

1. Chris challenged Andrew after Andrew talked about how well he could shoot free throws.

2. The ball bounced off the backboard.

3. Chris took his first shot after Andrew's first shot.

4. Andrew decided to get tips after Chris shot two free throws.

p. 45

Check that your paragraph is written in sequence.

Check that you have used time order words, such as first, next, and last.

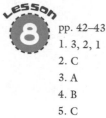

Unit 3

Working with Context

p. 47
2. C
3. C

LESSON 1 — pp. 48–49

1. B	9. A
2. C	10. C
3. D	11. A
4. A	12. C
5. B	13. D
6. D	14. B
7. C	15. B
8. D	16. C

LESSON 2 — pp. 50–51

1. D	9. B
2. B	10. D
3. C	11. D
4. D	12. A
5. A	13. D
6. D	14. A
7. C	15. D
8. A	16. C

LESSON 3 — pp. 52–53

1. C	9. D
2. B	10. A
3. C	11. B
4. A	12. D
5. A	13. B
6. C	14. C
7. C	15. A
8. B	16. C

LESSON 4 — pp. 54–55

1. D	9. A
2. C	10. B
3. C	11. A
4. D	12. D
5. B	13. B
6. A	14. D
7. A	15. C
8. C	16. D

LESSON 5 — pp. 56–57

1. C	5. C
2. D	6. B
3. C	7. C
4. D	8. D

LESSON 6 — pp. 58–59

1. C	5. C
2. C	6. A
3. A	7. C
4. A	8. D

LESSON 7 — pp. 60–61

1. A	5. D
2. B	6. D
3. C	7. A
4. B	8. B

LESSON 8 — pp. 62–63

1. B	5. D
2. B	6. A
3. D	7. D
4. A	8. C

Writing Roundup

p. 64
Possible answers include:
1. exciting or realistic
2. boring or silly
3. nervous or uncertain
4. performance or music
5. electricity or power
6. candles or flashlights

p. 65
Possible answers include

1. They could use rocks. They could use shell-shaped macaroni.

2. They could draw fish. They could use fish crackers.

3. They could paint the box. They could put sand in the box.

4. It might be horses. It might be the mayor's car.

5. It was a marching band. It was a group of clowns.

6. It was the circus animals. It was a float.

Unit 4

Practice Finding the Main Idea

p. 67

The correct answer is C. The paragraph tells about the front, sports, and comics sections of the newspaper.

LESSON 1 — pp. 68–69

1. B
2. B
3. C
4. C
5. A

LESSON 2 — pp. 70–71

1. C
2. A
3. B
4. B
5. A

LESSON 3 — pp. 72–73

1. D
2. B
3. A
4. C
5. B

LESSON 4 — pp. 74–75

1. C
2. C
3. A
4. A
5. B

LESSON 5 — pp. 76–77

1. B
2. C
3. A
4. A
5. D

LESSON 6 — pp. 78–79

1. D
2. B
3. B
4. C
5. A

LESSON 7 — pp. 80–81

1. B
2. D
3. B
4. A
5. A

LESSON 8 — pp. 82–83

1. D
2. B
3. C
4. A
5. D

Writing Roundup

p. 84
Possible answers include:

1. Birds never forget a food that made them sick.

2. A dead rattlesnake can be as dangerous as a live one.

3. A Comanche tribe in New Mexico provided the idea for semaphore.

p. 85

Check that you have underlined your main idea.

Check that you have used four details in your story.

Unit 5

Using What You Know

p. 87

geography, physical education, language, art

LESSON 1 pp. 88–89
1. C
2. C
3. B
4. A
5. D

LESSON 2 pp. 90–91
1. C
2. D
3. B
4. A
5. D

LESSON 3 pp. 92–93
1. C
2. B
3. B
4. C
5. A

LESSON 4 pp. 94–95
1. D
2. A
3. B
4. C
5. A

LESSON 5 pp. 96–97
1. B
2. A
3. C
4. D
5. A

LESSON 6 pp. 98–99
1. C
2. B
3. B
4. D
5. D

LESSON 7 pp. 100–101
1. D
2. D
3. A
4. A
5. B

LESSON 8 pp. 102–103
1. C
2. B
3. A
4. B
5. D

Writing Roundup

p. 104

Possible answers include:

1. Georgia Broadwick was a daring woman.

2. There probably aren't any $100,000 bills in use now.

3. Amalia likes listening to birds.

p. 105

Possible answers include:

1. No African American played in the major leagues in 1946. Jackie Robinson was the first African American to play in the major leagues in 1947.

2. Robinson was the only African American in the major leagues when he played his first game with the Dodgers. Dan Bankhead joined the Dodgers later in the year.

3. Bankhead was not a star with the Dodgers. He pitched in four games, and he was not with the Dodgers until the following year.

4. Robinson was a baseball star. He is in the Baseball Hall of Fame.

Unit 6

Practice Making Inferences

p. 107
2. A. F   B. F   C. I   D. I

LESSON 1 pp. 108–109
1. A. F   B. I   C. I   D. F
2. A. I   B. F   C. F   D. F
3. A. F   B. I   C. F   D. I
4. A. I   B. F   C. I   D. F
5. A. I   B. I   C. F   D. F

LESSON 2 pp. 110–111
1. A. F   B. F   C. I   D. F
2. A. F   B. I   C. F   D. I
3. A. I   B. F   C. I   D. F
4. A. I   B. F   C. F   D. F
5. A. F   B. F   C. I   D. I

LESSON 3 pp. 112–113
1. A. F   B. F   C. I   D. F
2. A. I   B. I   C. F   D. I
3. A. F   B. F   C. I   D. I
4. A. F   B. F   C. I   D. I
5. A. F   B. F   C. F   D. I

LESSON 4 pp. 114–115
1. A. F   B. I   C. I   D. I
2. A. F   B. I   C. F   D. I
3. A. I   B. F   C. I   D. F
4. A. F   B. I   C. I   D. F
5. A. F   B. F   C. I   D. F

LESSON 5 pp. 116–117
1. A. F   B. I   C. I   D. I
2. A. I   B. F   C. I   D. I
3. A. I   B. F   C. I   D. F
4. A. F   B. I   C. F   D. F
5. A. I   B. F   C. F   D. F

LESSON 6 pp. 118–119
1. A. I   B. I   C. I   D. F
2. A. F   B. F   C. I   D. I
3. A. F   B. F   C. I   D. I
4. A. I   B. F   C. F   D. I
5. A. F   B. F   C. I   D. F

LESSON 7 pp. 120–121
1. A. I   B. F   C. I   D. F
2. A. F   B. F   C. I   D. F
3. A. I   B. F   C. F   D. I
4. A. F   B. F   C. I   D. I
5. A. I   B. I   C. F   D. F

LESSON 8 pp. 122–123
1. A. F   B. I   C. F   D. I
2. A. I   B. I   C. F   D. I
3. A. I   B. F   C. I   D. I
4. A. I   B. I   C. I   D. I
5. A. I   B. F   C. F   D. I

Writing Roundup

p. 124

Possible answers include:

1. Carmela was wrapping a gift for her mother.

2. The tree needed water.

3. Yoko was in a post office or a store for mailing letters and packages.

p. 125

Possible answers include:

1. Bernardo is almost 70 years old.

2. Bernardo needed a ladder to reach cherries that he could not reach from the ground.

3. Bernardo is hard-working, weary, and lonely.

4. Keeping up the farm was too much work for one person.

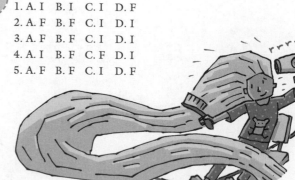